ROSEMARY DONEGAN

SPADINA AVENUE

INTRODUCTION BY RICK SALUTIN

DOUGLAS & McINTYRE VANCOUVER & TORONTO

Douglas & McIntyre Ltd.
1615 Venables Street
Vancouver, British Columbia V5L 2H1

Canadian Cataloguing in Publication Data

Donegan, Rosemary.
Spadina Avenue

Includes index.
ISBN 0-88894-472-1

1. Spadina Avenue (Toronto, Ont.). 2. Toronto
(Ont.) – Streets. I. Salutin, Rick, 1942-
II. Title.

FC3097.67.D66 1985   017.13'541   C85-099588-4
F1059.5.T68875S76 1985

Design: Michael Solomon
Typesetting: Spencer Brennan – Alphabets
Printed and bound in Canada by Friesen Printers

This publication has been partially
subsidized by Multiculturalism Canada,
Department of the Secretary of State.

SPADINA AVENUE

Contents

Toronto, 1883
The bird's eye view foreshortens Spadina on the left and idealizes the condition of the waterfront. The domed roundhouse and terminal elevator in the foreground are part of the Northern Railway yards. Union Station is on the right.
Newspaper engraving from *Canadian Illustrated News*, June 1, 1983, Public Archives Canada

Page 1:
Immigrants Arriving at Union Station, c. 1910
Pringle & Booth, Kelso Collection, Public Archives Canada (C 47042)

Page 2-3:
Queen and Spadina, April, 1921
William James, City of Toronto Archives (7338)

Page 4:
Gateway to Spadina, 1981
Looking north from Wellington, the Balfour and Tower buildings form a gateway at Adelaide and Spadina.
Peter MacCallum

Page 5:
Street Scene, 1950's
Camden and Spadina, looking east to the Spadina Building.
Kenny Collection, Fisher Rare Book Room, University of Toronto (Box 63, 179)

Preface

Spadina Avenue, the place, has always fascinated me, with its width, its bizarre assortment of shops, bars and the music. The name, which I first came across as Spadina Crescent in Saskatoon, also has an unusual cadence, whether pronounced "spa-DIE-na" or "spa-DEE-na." In 1982, while researching the Spadina Expressway, I began to find photographs, from the early 1900's, of an elegant treed street with a centre boulevard and handsome buildings. At first glance they didn't look at all like the street I was familiar with. Yet on closer inspection I discovered that the street hadn't really changed that much. Gradually, a series of images of times, events and buildings started to emerge. Although the pictures themselves weren't continuous or chronological, they documented the layers of social, political and cultural events that make up urban social history.

The project, documenting the history of Spadina Avenue, evolved out of my interest in examining the photography of a public street from the perspective of urban culture and politics of the 1980's. What made the research so captivating was the combination of local popular history, the architecture of the street and its location on the western edge of the city's central core. Since the 1920's, Spadina has suffered from benign neglect, which has allowed it to develop on its own terms — whatever they were. But more recently, it exists under intense pressure as land prices skyrocket and development interests move west from the central core of the city into the fragile garment district.

The exhibition, "SPADINA AVE: A Photohistory," which opened at A SPACE Gallery in August, 1984, was the initial result of my

research. This book, with Rick Salutin's help, evolved out of the exhibition.

All of the scattered stories and pictures in this book could not have been brought together without those individual people and movements who "lived out" part of their lives on Spadina. Their affection for the street and its popular mythology is not simply an exercise in nostalgia — looking back to the "good old days." The 1920's and 30's, when the seeds of Spadina's cultural traditions were sown, was a time when daily life was more coherent. Work, politics and culture were more integrated and operated locally. There were fewer choices, but they were major ones over language, family, work, politics and eventually war — the choices that shape history.

In the process of researching Spadina Avenue, I talked to and interviewed hundreds of people and looked at thousands of photographs. I hope that I have evoked their history with the respect and integrity that is its due. For it is the people that I interviewed, who loaned photographs and shared their ideas and their families' histories, who are the source of this book.

A great amount of work, both paid and volunteer, was involved in the original exhibition, and I would like to thank all those individuals and friends who helped in the mounting and installation of the exhibition. Peter MacCallum's personal commitment and expertise as a photographer provided the visual framework for the exhibition and this book. The support of those at A SPACE, a contemporary artists' gallery that had recently moved to Spadina, indicated their commitment to a local history and their own part in it.

I would like to personally thank: Ruth Frager and Craig Heron for sharing their historical knowledge and support, Barry Sampson for his innovative furniture and installation design, Stan Denniston for his expertise in mounting and installing the photographs, Renee Baert and Dinah Forbes for their assistance in the production and editing of the textual material.

The historical photographs which form the core of this book were located with the expertise and assistance of the archival staffs of the City of Toronto Archives, the Toronto Jewish Congress Archives, the Baldwin Room of the Metro Reference Library, the Multicultural History Society Collection at the Ontario Archives and the Public Archives of Canada.

The research and production of the exhibition, and by extension this book, were assisted by the Canada Council, the MacLean Foundation, the Ontario Heritage Foundation, Secretary of State: Multiculturalism Canada and the Ontario Bicentennial Celebrations, Toronto Arts Council, Toronto Sesquicentennial Ward 6 Committee and Wintario.

I would like to thank Rick Salutin for his evocative introduction to Spadina Avenue as a public/private place, where fragments of all our lives are left. And finally, I wish to pay respect to and thank all the photographers, named and anonymous, who have contributed to this book. For it is their individual photographs that give meaning to the collective memory of Spadina Avenue as a street and a public place.

Rosemary Donegan
1985

7

Introduction

Everyone takes his own walk along Spadina. It's that kind of street. People feel affectionate, or intense, or nostalgic. It evokes a reaction, something personal, a relationship. The relationship differs for each person, each generation, each ethnic community. That's the kind of street it is.

Even Spadina's name sets it apart from other Toronto streets. It suggests a different way of regarding the world. Some street names are straightforward. They tell where they go, like Front, or Bay. Others pay homage to authority: King, Queen, Parliament; or to respectable institutions like Church and University. Many conjure up images of powerful people from another society: British lords like Dufferin, or dukes like Richmond. British ministers of war like Bathurst and Bloor and Yonge; British prime ministers like Wellington and Gladstone. In fact, there are probably more streets in this city that remind us of somewhere else than of what we have here. One of our literary critics says that Canadians always ask the question, Where Is Here? No wonder.

This displacement (literally) doesn't hold for the city's own name. There are no Torontos in Sussex, Wessex or Essex, though there is a York, as Toronto used to be called. Toronto is a Huron word that means "place of meeting," probably because of the two rivers that empty into the lake here, and because of the sheltered harbour the Islands provide. Spadina is a word in the Ojibway language. It's practically the only street name in the city that recalls Toronto's original inhabitants. Maybe that's why wave after wave of immigrants have felt comfortable on Spadina.

Many Toronto street names (and other local features) imply that the city is still the preserve of modern descendants of groups like the United Empire Loyalists or the Family Compact. (They even have some street names of their own: Jarvis, Beverley, Ryerson.) Spadina, though, reminds almost everyone that they're newcomers in a place where all non-native Ojibway-speakers have only recently arrived. It's an equalizer.

Everyone starts his walk along Spadina some place different. Some set out at the foot near the lake. Others at the top, by the Crescent, or even at the "Y." Others still at an intersection — College, Dundas, Queen. Someone comes east along Kensington from the Market; someone else west along Cecil. There are those who go up one side of the street and down the other. Or cross over. Some just hang out on their corner.

Dr. William Baldwin probably didn't walk much on Spadina. He'd have ridden it on horseback or in his carriage, perhaps accompanied by son Robert, who went on to become the architect of responsible government — an overrated Canadian achievement. Actually, when Baldwin arrived at the start of the nineteenth century, there *was* no Spadina — just a marked-off western boundary for the town site of York. Along the edge of York large land plots had been granted to transplanted members of the British gentry. Among them was Peter Russell, president of the

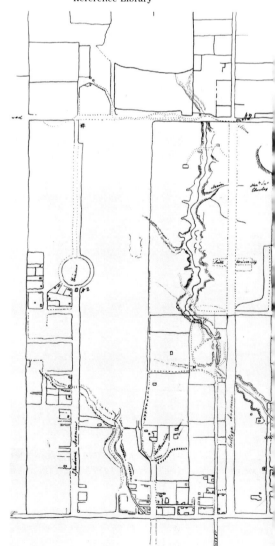

Toronto, 1838, Royal Engineer's Survey
History Department, Metro Reference Library

8

carefully vetted legislature of Upper Canada and successor to John Graves Simcoe, first lieutenant-governor of the colony. Baldwin, who was a lawyer and a doctor, became the Russells' family physician, married one of the daughters and inherited a piece of the estate, well north of the lake along that western boundary.

The town, then as now, spread north from the Lake Ontario shore. Along the way the ground rose slightly, almost imperceptibly; today you only notice the grade if you are riding a bicycle. After several miles, far past the limits of settlement in those days and well into the bush, came a steep ascent just above the meandering line that is now Davenport Road. It marked the original shoreline of the lake before the glacier retreated. It's called Lake Iroquois in that incarnation. Here on the Davenport Hill, Baldwin built a home and called it Ishtadinauh — "gradual rise of land."

From his hill, Baldwin could look out on a fine vista all the way to the lake. Perhaps one day he pictured a road — no, a broad avenue lined with trees — leading right to his door. Between 1813 and 1818 he laid it out, 131 feet wide. It was later widened to 160. This made it over twice the width of streets like Yonge, Bloor and Lot (later Queen). Who knows why Baldwin made his street so wide? Maybe as an early attempt to enhance property values; certainly during the nineteenth century many fine homes were constructed along Baldwin's avenue. Perhaps it was just a quirk. At any rate, the results were profound.

The width of Spadina meant the street itself dominated buildings on either side of it. The life of the street focussed on the *street*, and on the people in it. Other downtown streets seem to exist as an occasion for buildings, which hide people away inside them. On Spadina, buildings become a border for the street, which displays the people. That expanse of street also provided an arena for crowds, marches or protests, whenever those people in the street had opinions or emotions to express.

Baldwin also designed a circle just above what is now College, and he deeded it to the city as a park in 1838. This was just after the violent rebellion of 1837; perhaps he meant it as a symbol of reconciliation. Meanwhile at its other end Spadina was extended from Queen Street south to Front, so that the soldiers at Fort York could be moved quickly into the city in case there was more trouble. The extension was called Brock Street for the next fifty years.

The broad avenue itself never made it up to Baldwin's home on the hill. It petered out or rather narrowed into an ordinary-sized street once it passed Bloor. Nor does Baldwin's house exist anymore. Just as well. It would have been overshadowed by the comic presence of Casa Loma on that same hill. As for souvenirs of Baldwin on the thoroughfare he envisaged, there is only one: a little corner where modest Baldwin Street empties into teeming Spadina Avenue.

I start my own walk at Spadina and Adelaide. On the southwest corner, the Darling Building towers. My father told me it was the first fireproof building in Toronto.

Dr. William W. Baldwin, c. 1850
A lithograph from a painting by Theophile Hamel.
Baldwin Room, Metro Reference Library (T 31037)

Repaving Bed for Street-car Tracks, August, 1937
Public works photograph, City
of Toronto Archives (RDY 1444)

When I snickered, he said that was very important in the
early days of the century, because it lowered insurance
costs.

Factories filled the upper floors, in the rear basement
was Darling Lunch, and at street level — 100 Spadina —
the sign over the door read A. Salutin and Brothers. For
forty-six years. No retail, it said inside the window. Stairs
led down a half-flight to the dress racks presided over by
the Ontario agents for Montreal dressmakers like Lady
Fair (half-sizes), Bel-Mar (wedding gowns) and, in the final
days of the partnership, Wendy Originals.

My brother and I thought of them as the Marx brothers
of the dress business: Abe and Harry and Saul. They were
from another age when families were close-knit and went
into business together.

Abe was oldest. He occupied a massive swivel armchair
in front of a cluttered rolltop desk and puffed cigars.
"*Hel*-lo," he'd boom into the phone. Harry, next in line,
had a swivel chair but no arms, before an ordinary desk
piled high with accounts he plunged into as he rolled up
his sleeves and punched a push-button ballpoint pen. He
was my bachelor uncle who'd gone to war and been
wounded. I found it hard to connect that gallant past to
his careful present. Beyond his desk in an ordinary
straight-backed chair against the wall sat Saul, my dad,
the youngest Salutin brother. In another chair, between
the two desks, sat Grandpa — most of the time. He hadn't
worked as a cutter since his eyesight faded. He didn't do
anything in the office, but his boys kept him on salary.

The door above would swing open and a buyer would
pause at the top like the Queen stepping out of her plane
and hesitating a moment to recall which Commonwealth
country she'd landed in. Then the buyer would descend
the stairs, greeting everyone below — including Grandpa

— and hailed in turn by the Salutins. Then a brother would spring into action (depending on whose customer it was), escorting the buyer among the dress racks, yanking one model after another from the pack and spreading it with the lower hand while hoisting it with the upper. "This one's a runner," he'd say. They sold those garments for half a century, and I don't believe any of them ever thought about dresses as things of beauty or function that women wore in real life. They were "numbers" ordered by buyers and shipped late (inevitably) by manufacturers.

Dining Room, Spadina Hotel, 1950's
Spadina Hotel

Uncle Harry died in 1973. Dad and Uncle Abe carried on together for awhile. Those were Dad's glory years. He came into his own with the Wendy line. Many of my friends had Wendys in their closets. In 1978 the remaining Salutin brothers split up and for the first time Dad got an office of his own. It was at King and Bathurst, an easy walk from Spadina. When people asked if they'd had a fight, I'd say, Yes — every day for forty-six years.

I amble south toward the lake. A block from the Darling Building, corner of King, is the Spadina Hotel. It's been a Toronto fixture even longer than the Darling Building. I try to remember the first time I went in. Ten years ago — more. I was with my dad.

The night before we'd held a typical slanging match. I was talking to my mother on the phone. In the background I could hear him fuming. "Put that idiot on the line," I told her. "Why don't you stop bellowing like a wounded elephant," I said to him. "I'm not wounded and I'm not an elephant," he bellowed. It was the kind of exchange that had marked our relationship all the way back to my final years in high school. For some reason we decided to have lunch together the next day — something we'd never done before. Maybe it was simple boredom with the *status quo*. We agreed to meet on Spadina.

The next day at noon we hunched over a red-checked tablecloth in the dining-room of the Spadina Hotel — his choice. It might have been the set of a 1940's movie. I thought back to other shared meals — happy lunches at Zuchter's deli the summer I worked for him as a shipper, while my friends went to their cottages. Or farther back. Dad was taking me to the bus for Camp Northland — my first time away from home. We stopped at the Crescent Grill for breakfast. It was jammed. I throbbed and sobbed, tears dripped into my orange juice. "What's the matter, Solly? Doesn't he want to go?" said a salesman behind us at the counter. "Sure he does," beamed my father. "He's really happy about it!" We had a history on this street.

Over lunch, he told me he agreed with the harsh things he knew I felt about him. I was stunned. I'd never imagined he'd say such a thing, or even think it. He said he wished he could make it up to me. I said I didn't care about making up anything, only about doing better in the future. *He* looked stunned. We talked about the past — not our own father-and-son past, but *his* story, and his family's. Where my grandparents had come from in Russia, how they'd come here, why there were no other Salutins anywhere in the world. I was fascinated. We argued. Not about guilt (his) or disrespect (mine). About

11

the world: Trudeau, Quebec, Vietnam, the economy. People at nearby tables — buyers, manufacturers, models, designers — glanced at us as they ate. The red-faced father in the *shmatah* trade and his radical son — a professor, maybe a writer — arguing as those two generations were bound to do, playing out roles they were made for. Such a shock — we were talking!

Thanks to Spadina. We were not at home — that amorphous place, more myth than fact, full of ancient and unresolvable feelings. We were on Spadina where he knew who he was, and so did everyone else. A crackerjack salesman, one of the Salutin boys from the centre of the universe, Spadina and Adelaide. He existed there as a person, not just as my father, and by the time we started into the short ribs and mashed potatoes, even I had got the message.

I continue south to Wellington, southwest corner. McGregor Hosiery, home of Happy Foot socks. I've stood here at 6:30 in the morning handing leaflets to yawning workers as they trudge from the bus to the employees' entrance. It's one of the last big factories left on Spadina. The rest have absconded to industrial parks in the suburbs, where every factory has a squat anonymity. McGregor is still owned by the Lipson family, tough and competent bosses. Where did they get that *name*? I picture the founders years ago, the Lipson brothers, speaking with heavy Yiddish accents — probably speaking Yiddish for that matter — saying, "Let's call it something that sounds *really* Canadian. What about — McGregor!"

I helped organize that plant in the mid-1970's, when I worked with a textile union. It was a typical drive for a medium-sized factory with about two hundred workers. We met one day at a nearby coffee shop with the people who'd contacted the union: Cyril Singh, a Guyanese in the shipping department, and Natalie Benevides, a nineteen-year-old Portuguese single mother who was a "finisher." Cyril knew Natalie because he sold Avon products as a sideline, and he'd recruited her to help. They told us about McGregor and we told them what had to be done: sign people up, get the names and addresses of anyone you're not sure will support the union — and keep it quiet. We made visits in the evenings, to the usual mix: Portuguese, West Indians, East Indians, Greeks, Italians,

Chinese, a few "Canadians." Mainly women. We explained how safe it was to sign a union card, how the law protected their identity, and they said, "Sure sure, but the boss will know. He knows everything."

The company didn't catch on at first. They had probably underestimated their workers' capacity for secrecy and guile. When someone eventually told them, they got (a) nice (everyone received a thirty-cent raise) and (b) nasty (foreladies hinted that people could be arrested and deported for union membership). Most of the women came from the Portuguese Azores; they couldn't *vote* there, much less join a union. The drive slowed. Cyril had left the plant by then. The company had offered him a promotion into management and he'd felt he could neither accept nor refuse. I last saw him playing a sitar on a cable TV show. Then Natalie was fired. The union charged the company at the Ontario labour board. The drive stopped. Workers waited to see what this union could *really* do against the boss.

When the case finally went before the board, the company lawyer attacked Natalie. He said the only reason she'd got involved with the union was to meet men. Hadn't she been seen kissing Cyril Singh on the elevator? The boss's son, who'd recently taken over, looked on. He was in his forties: tanned, fit, blow-dried, aviator glasses. Natalie said this was not a love affair; it was a union affair. She held her own in an unfamiliar language. The board ordered her reinstated with back pay. The drive picked up and the union won certification after more than a year. When I described it, friends asked, "Didn't that all go out in the thirties?" "Nope," I said. "It was a typical organizing campaign." Well, not quite typical. There was a twist. It seems there's always a twist when there's a connection to Spadina. Sometimes I feel there's a natural tendency for everything on Spadina to flow together: personal, political, professional. Sometimes I feel like everything that happens on Spadina reminds me of my life, and everything in my life happened on Spadina.

In the case of McGregor, I had a friend. She had a fine,

Colin Linden, Local Musician, September, 1984
Ben Mark Holzberg

Clarence Square from the North Side, 1886
Watercolour by Robert J. Wylie, Royal Ontario Museum (949.150.8)

CLARENCE SQUARE
~ FROM NORTH SIDE ~

all-Canadian quality: ruddy, athletic, wide-eyed; but there was a sadness about her. She had been married and had left her husband and children in their home in the suburbs. One day she asked if I'd like a colour TV set; she didn't use hers. I took it and got hooked on colour. Then suddenly she needed it back; someone was spending time with her and she wanted to re-furnish. He was a Jewish businessman, she said. I carted the TV over glumly, went into severe withdrawal and hastily bought the set I still have. Months later she told me happily that they were marrying, buying a townhouse, she thought she might convert to Judaism. "What does he do, exactly?" I asked as we parted. "He owns a factory," she said. "They make socks." Later that week the union office called and said it had contacts at McGregor who wanted to organize. My friend and I haven't talked much since then.

There's not much point in going farther south. I'm almost at the end of the street. Down at Front, in the early 1900's, there was a building for the British Welcome League. I guess they tried desperately to homogenize the hordes of immigrants congregating on Spadina. Now it's a body-shop and car rental agency. Beyond, over the railway lands and down by the lakefront, they're building condos. I don't think condos can be considered part of Spadina. They should be disqualified.

Or should they? I look across the street from McGregor to elegant Clarence Square, with its Georgian terraced houses. Exquisite, elitist. They've been there for over a century, since well before the factories and the flood of immigrants. A city planner told me the tenants' association there serves Scotch at its meetings.

I decide to go back up to Adelaide and walk north. Kitty-corner from the Darling Building is the Balfour Building. A factory inside was the location for a TV film I once wrote about immigrant women unionizing and about the father and son who own the company and try to stop them. The film's producers thought no owner would offer his shop after seeing the script, but there was one — his father-in-law had founded the company. He saw the old man as the hero of the piece. He even brought his mother-in-law to watch, the day we shot a scene in which the boss harangues his employees about the dangers of a union.

Spadina is about continuity between generations. Children take over from parents, the family connection counts. Once on this corner my brother hailed me. He'd just completed a degree in criminology. "Maybe we should take over the office," he said. "We're the only Salutin brothers left."

I continue north. Camden. Richmond. Then Queen.

Here at the junction with Queen, Spadina sends out impulses in both directions. Queen Street West has acquired its own personality in the past ten years. Performance artists, alternate galleries, clubs, bookstores, nouvelle cuisine and vegetarian restaurants — beside the old shops and appliance stores, the goulash and pool halls. The new personality of Queen West isn't ethnic or industrial in the Spadina tradition. But it is, in that tradition,

Arasha Nodelman, Presser, T. Eaton Co., c. 1916
Multicultural History Society, Ontario Archives (MSR 9171)

quirky and individualistic. The bookstores and eating-places aren't Coles or McDonald's. There is, shall we say, a family connection to these east and west offshoots. Spadina itself continues north and so do I.

In 1911, just after my grandfather arrived in Canada and started work, he went on strike along with 1,200 other garment workers against the T. Eaton Company. Then, and for decades after, Eaton's ran a huge clothing factory in Toronto. It employed seventy-five per cent of Ontario's cloakmakers who made the clothes Eaton's sold across Canada. ("You couldn't see from one end to the other," said my father of a visit twenty-five years later, when he and my grandfather were filling contracts for Eaton's themselves.)

In 1910 Eaton's introduced a new system for sewing in linings by machine. This "technological change" meant loss of jobs. The workers went out for eighteen weeks.

The company brought scab labour from England, the United States and elsewhere in Canada. The workers set up twenty-four-hour picket lines, demonstrated and created a system of community relief. Eighty per cent were Jewish. Jewish women collected money publicly for the strikers. The city declared their action illegal.

Despite the strike, the new system was introduced, and jobs were lost. The strikers returned to work. My father, who was one year old at the time, heard the tale in later years. He says one condition laid down for the return was that there be no demonstration by the workers. Nevertheless as they re-entered the plant a shout went up. In retaliation Eaton's fired a number of strike leaders, my grandfather among them.

Those let loose by Eaton's, and those fired, had to support their families. Some managed to establish small manufacturing operations of their own, and others worked for them. My grandfather spent the rest of his active years alternately working for others to gather a little capital, then "setting up" for himself where, according to family lore, he sweated other workers as harshly as he had ever been treated himself. He was such a poor businessman that he inevitably went bankrupt and had to go back to work for someone else until he could set up again...and so forth.

Eaton's near-monopoly of the clothing industry was to some extent broken by the largely unsuccessful strike. It remained dominant, though, through a system of contracting-out, and because of its huge market. To set up independently, only enough capital was required to buy a couple of "Singers" (the Model T of sewing machines), a press iron and some material. The first new plants were located in old houses and mansions along Adelaide, Richmond and Queen, on either side of Spadina. Their original owners had left and moved north while immigrants — Germans and then Jews — came into the area. The plants would contain one small factory on the main floor and another on the upper floor. Gradually Spadina itself became the centre of the trade; activity spread along the

Sewing Loft, 1910's
United Church Archives

15

Avenue as far north as Dundas. Shops opened and closed
constantly. A directory for 1926, for instance, shows the
A&S Skirt Co. — Uncle Abe and Uncle Harry — on Spadina between Phoebe and Sullivan. This was a dummy —
my grandfather using his sons' names to reopen after
another bankruptcy. Up the street, just below Dundas,
Uncle Moe was supposedly making hats. It was the era of
industrial Spadina.

The age of industrial Spadina was also the age of Jewish
Spadina. Between 1901 and 1931 the population of Toronto grew by four times, from 156,000 to 631,000. The
Jewish population grew *fifteen* times in the same years,
from 3,000 to 45,000, as the Jewish masses of Eastern
Europe crossed the Atlantic. Their arrival tended (in the
eyes of some, threatened) to change the city's character.
   In 1901 ninety per cent of Toronto's citizens had their
roots in Britain. The largest ethnic group were Germans
(three per cent); the next largest were Jews at 1.9 per
cent. By 1931 Jews had become by far the largest non-
British group at 7.2 per cent (Italians were second at 2.1
per cent); the city at large had become eighty per cent
British. It was change enough to rouse intense hostile
reaction. In 1924 the Toronto *Telegram* wrote, "An influx
of Jews puts a worm next the kernal of every fair city
where they get hold. These people have no national tradition....They engage in the wars of no country, but flit

Labor Lyceum Stock
Certificate, 1929
Al Hercovitch

from one to another under passports changed with cha-
meleon swiftness, following up the wind the smell of
lucre.''

As late as the 1951 census, Jews still comprised the
largest ethnic component of Toronto at six per cent, with
Ukrainians second at 3.5 per cent. By this time the British
were down to seventy per cent — still a substantial majority — and the Jewish era on Spadina was coming to an
end. Jews moved north as other immigrants established
themselves on the Avenue.

During the first half of this century the city was
bursting. New energies had arrived with the power to
transform things. For the first time Toronto was not
entirely dominated by people with roots in the United
Kingdom. But the "British" remained a large enough
majority (more than two-thirds even at mid-century) that
they continued to set the city's tone. Toronto retained its
starchy, puritanical, Orange character. In many ways it
still does.

The encroaching wave — so sinister and un-British —
stood no chance of taking over. They had to be content
with asserting themselves in their own areas, above all
Spadina. Since Jews were the largest element in that
wave during the first half of the century, they had a
special role in the development of the city. The mix of
industrial Spadina and Jewish Spadina was volatile and
creative.

"It was a militant centre!" says J.B. Salsberg. Everything about working life on Spadina led to feistiness and
confrontation. "You had to strike," adds the former Communist member of the legislature. "You had to form
unions and then you had to strike again." Those conflicts
pre-dated the formalization of modern labour procedures.
Organizing campaigns were often spontaneous, and contracts were easily ignored. Many jobs on Spadina involved
piecework: workers were paid according to the quantity
they produced, rather than hourly. They'd manage to fix
a price per garment with their employer, divide it up
among themselves, then suddenly find he'd changed the
pattern and a whole new set of prices were required. A
lot of "chiselling" went on. The employer would
dramatically announce he had a customer, but at a lower
price than usual, and he'd press the workers to agree or
lose the work altogether. Since many plants were small,
and many bosses were former workers, and virtually
everybody was Jewish, a personal quality often per-
meated the conflicts. Because everyone lived nearby, a
strike affected the local storekeepers and tradesmen, who
wouldn't be paid until the dispute was settled. In a sense,
as Salsberg says, "the whole community went on strike."

Unions proliferated. The Amalgamated Clothing Workers, the Capmakers' Union, the International Ladies' Garment Workers, the Millinery Workers, the Fur Workers. In
1928 they formed a co-op, sold shares at five dollars each
and built the Labor Lyceum on Spadina two blocks north
of Dundas. For forty years it was the centre of labour
activity on the street.

Experience in the workplace led to broader questions.

Thou Shalt Remember
Storefront poster advertis-
ing a benefit performance
for the Jewish Old Folks
Home on Cecil Street.
Stella Rudolph (nee Barsh)

17

People challenged the *status quo* for a multitude of reasons. "I became a Communist because I was a Jew," says Joshua Gershman, for many years editor of the *Wochenblatt*, a Yiddish-Communist newspaper whose office was at Spadina and King. The Communists were one of many left-wing political groups. The Workmen's Circle at first contained all of them. At its Toronto convention in 1922 it expelled supporters of what would become the Communist party. Throughout the world at that time socialists were divided over the meaning of the Russian Revolution. In 1924 the Canadian Communist party was formed; fifty per cent of its members were Finns, twenty per cent were Ukrainians, and fifteen per cent were Jews — many of whom lived and worked on Spadina.

Each force on Spadina seemed to add vitality to the Jewish community rather than fragment it. People continued to observe their religion. They built new synagogues and expanded old ones. Cultural organizations flourished: Yiddish theatre, Yiddish literature. Spadina became a centre for every kind of opposition and alternative to the sober Upper Canadian mainstream: economic, political, cultural, ethnic, linguistic.

The Depression intensified these relations. Unemployment doubled between 1929 and 1930. By 1931 wages were below what they had been ten years earlier. Many workers grew dissatisfied with the conservatism of their traditional leadership. They began forming new unions with an industrial form of organization and a more militant approach. The Industrial Union of Needle Trades Workers organized among the dressmakers on Spadina. It was part of the Communist-led Workers' Unity League. The older conservative unions responded to the mood of their members and to the threat of competition. In 1931 the Cloakmakers' Union of the International Ladies' Garment Workers Union called a general strike on Spadina — a new tactic. At ten o'clock on a Tuesday morning workers began to pour out of the shops large and small. "Within fifteen or twenty minutes," says organizer Bernard Shane, "Spadina Avenue became black with workers." They streamed to strike headquarters at the Labor Lyceum.

There was another industry-wide strike in 1933, followed by a general contract. In 1934 one of the largest companies, Superior Cloak, closed its Spadina factory and moved to Guelph to escape the union. Such "runaway shops" had become common in Quebec. The union sent car pools and busses with picketers to Guelph. They battled the Guelph police. The new plant shut down and the company had to reopen in Toronto. The next year legislation regulating pay, hours of work and a minimum wage was passed.

The left-wing groups and parties also responded to the Depression. At street corners up and down Spadina, orators challenged the system, the establishment, the ruling class, capitalism, the banks, the monopolies. The Toronto establishment replied in their fashion. In 1929 the board of police commissioners banned all public addresses not in

Man Under Arrest, c. 1931
Toronto Telegram, Canada Wide

Eight Men Speak Poster,
December, 1933
Design and woodcuts by
Rick Taylor.
Toby Gordon Ryan

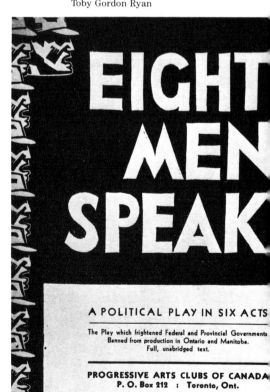

EIGHT MEN SPEAK

A POLITICAL PLAY IN SIX ACTS

The Play which frightened Federal and Provincial Governments
Banned from production in Ontario and Manitoba.
Full, unabridged text.

PROGRESSIVE ARTS CLUBS OF CANADA
P. O. Box 212 : Toronto, Ont.

TWENTY CENTS IN CANADA : THIRTY CENTS ABROAD

Anti-Hitler Demonstration, Queen's Park, July, 1933
Toronto Telegram, Canada Wide

English. They stripped licences from anyone who rented
space to "Communist or Bolshevik public meetings."
Mayor McBride (of the Islands ferry by the same name)
said, "Our stopping of Communist meetings shows that we
are truly British." "Communist" and "Bolshevik" by these
lights were catch-all terms for any radical opposition,
especially voiced in a foreign tongue. The *Globe & Mail*
editorialized that though not all Jews were Communists,
all Communists were Jews.

Deportation was a political weapon. After 1919 anyone
not born in Canada could be deported for advocating the
overthrow of authority by force, no matter how long he'd
been in the country. Those in Canada for under five years
could be deported as "public charges" with no trial. In
1930 four thousand people were expelled; in 1931, seven
thousand.

That year eight leaders of the Communist party were
arrested under a section of the criminal code prohibiting
advocacy of violent overthrow of the government. They
were tried and imprisoned. The case became a touchstone
for civil liberties activity across Canada. In 1933, at the
Standard Theatre on Spadina, the Progressive Arts Club
presented a play called *Eight Men Speak* — a defence of
the imprisoned men. It attacked the police and the courts.
Its first performance sold out. A second was scheduled,
but the police commission threatened to revoke the
theatre's licence. In 1934 the eight were released from
prison in Kingston.

Spadina also responded to events in Europe, especially
the rise of Nazism. In July, 1933, fifteen thousand people
marched up the Avenue to protest the anti-semitism of
the new German government. They gathered in Clarence
Square — all the needle trade unions, over fifty Jewish
organizations, along with many English-speaking and
international groups. They proceeded to Queen's Park. It
was probably the largest demonstration Toronto had seen.

By May Day, 1938, the same united front, stronger and
larger, included Communists, the CCF and the Trades and
Labour Congress. It brought twenty-five thousand people
to Queen's Park. They chanted, "Make Toronto a Union

19

Town" and condemned the "Hepburn-Duplessis Axis," neatly including the leaders of Ontario and Quebec with those of world fascism. In the cauldron of the thirties all issues — economic exploitation, union rights, free speech, political dissent, anti-semitism, fascism — tended to merge and conflate. In Toronto, Spadina was the centre of action and concern. At the end of the decade the whole heady mix exploded and transformed.

The Second World War marked a watershed for Spadina. In a way it lanced the boil of Spadina as a centre of opposition. Business picked up, particularly because of military orders. Uncle Abe has hinted at fortunes made on the Avenue by cutting corners, or deals. He semi-apologized that the Salutin brothers didn't join in. Between those like Uncle Harry, who joined the army, and those hired for the step-up in manufacturing, unemployment pretty well disappeared.

Political and social tensions diminished, even reversed. Governments and unions reached agreements, including no-strike pledges, to keep industry working. The Jewish population enthusiastically supported the war against Nazism. Even Communists who had been banned and interned at the start of the war became discreet government backers when the Soviet Union and the Allies joined against Hitler. In 1943 party labour chief J.B. Salsberg was elected to the provincial legislature in a riding that amounted to Spadina. He held the seat for twelve years.

Right after the war, the Jewish community began a major shift. It had been a largely working-class, left-wing society. It became increasingly wealthy and — though this was more gradual — politically conservative. By the 1951 census Canadian Jews ranked highest in average annual income of any ethnic category including "British." In 1955 J.B. Salsberg was challenged in the provincial election by another Jew — insurance agent Allan Grossman, running for the Tories! The entire community divided in a vituperative campaign. Salsberg was red-baited, Grossman was called "the Jewish fascist." Grossman won and went on to become a cabinet minister.

Jews were leaving Spadina and moving north — sometimes just up Spadina itself to Forest Hill Village; sometimes farther to Bathurst Heights, Bathurst Manor, Bayview, Don Mills. Neat, suburban, unethnic communities in which life revolved around shopping plazas instead of factories, and there were no street corners. On Spadina the Jewish-owned factories and businesses still operated, and on Wednesday afternoons the buyers still buzzed around, but there were fewer and fewer Jewish workers *in* the factories. More recent immigrants replaced them. The unions were still led by Jews, but the members were often Italian, Greek and Portuguese. Jewish diners still filled Shopsy's, Switzer's and United Bakers for lunch, and many people still drove down from their homes in the suburbs to eat in familiar surroundings. But they were also taking exploratory forays to Lichee Gardens for chow mein, and Vesuvio's for pizza. The industrial, Jewish era was ending on Spadina.

Campaign Leaflets for the J.B. Salsberg Election Committee
Kenny Collection, Fisher Rare Book Room, University of Toronto

Victory Burlesque, "Home of Girlesk," 1950's
Canadian Tribune, Public Archives Canada (PA 93559, 935561, 935562)

Standing here at the corner of Spadina and Dundas, looking back down what once was the heart of the garment district — itself the heart of Spadina life — it is easy to become nostalgic. At the other end of this stretch, A. Salutin and Brothers is no more. Over near Bathurst Dad has an office but no line. The world isn't crying out for a seventy-five-year-old salesman of young women's dresses, so he sublets to a young Jewish trader who spends half the year in the Far East.

There's still production activity down that strip, but nothing like there once was. Imports have cut heavily into the Canadian market and, to tell the truth, the *shmatah* business has become something of a pariah in the eyes of government policy-makers and experts. "We're going to stop propping up mature industries that will never be competitive in this generation, like clothing, textiles, footwear," scowled one minister in charge of trade recently. There's a near-irrational hatred of the garment industry in such circles. They see it as backward, almost an embarrassment — something that belongs in the low-wage countries of southeast Asia, which they count on to fill most of Canada's clothing needs in coming years. (They make exceptions in the case of high-priced lines of apparel meant for wealthier buyers here and abroad.) In place of these "mature" industries (a patronizing term which makes you think of our scandalous treatment of the elderly) they have a vision of a new economy based on high technology: microchips, transistors, Canadarms for U.S. space vehicles.

The vision is, to say the least, questionable. After all, what is really wrong with a nation doing the honest work of clothing itself? Food, clothing, housing — these remain the basic human needs and their provision lends a dignity to the work of those who do it. As for fantasies of a hi-tech economy, there is no evidence to suggest it can become a significant Canadian reality. The mindset has a religious quality — Heaven (as hi-tech) and Hell (as Spadina). Spadina the Outsider: unrespectable, frowned on by the Canadian establishment and those who propagate the official view of things in our society. So Spadina isn't fashionable. So what else is new?

21

What is it that really aggravates the gurus of hi-tech when they think of the garment industry? What is their image of it? What is the image any of us have of the garment industry? Probably the worker with his/her product. The finished piece of work is not separate from the person finishing it off. The workers are visibly present in the production process. That's the practical meaning of "labour-intensive." What is the image of a hi-tech industry? A shining production process which almost seems to happen by itself. Perhaps there's a boss, a creative, risk-taking entrepreneur out on the frontier of the new technology. A few discreet technicians drift in and out of the picture. But there are no workers! Can this be the profound emotional appeal of hi-tech? Maybe in the minds of hi-tech visionaries the Canadian economy of the future simply functions — a bureaucrat's dream — with no human beings at all!

In contrast — Spadina! The *shmatah* business. Redolent of the work-life of the nineteenth century — the 1930's at the latest. Sweatshops — still. Bosses and workers — human beings all — in incessant and often personal conflict. Strikes. Homework. *Piecework*.

Piecework sums up everything that seems archaic about old industrial Spadina. Workers pushed and harried so the boss can extract the equivalent of two hours of work for one extra hour of pay — and gain the edge to keep his company alive in a hellishly competitive industry. Piecework was an issue in the Eaton's strike of 1911. A 1935 royal commission reported that piecework kept workers on Spadina below minimum wage while creating "nerve strain." It has always been connected with the most backward, dirty, labour-intensive and immigrant-serviced sectors of the economy. It seems the complete contradiction of the sanitized world of hi-tech.

Yet the contradiction seems, more than it is. Piecework on Spadina has already entered the age of computerization. Industrial engineers have evolved a jargon which breaks down the component moves of any factory task. They feed it into a computer and a "normal" rate emerges in indisputable International Units (I.U.'s), including an allotment for P.F.D. (Personal Fatigue and Downtime). Workers can no longer resist by conspiring to work at an agreed pace while the time-study man looks on; they face the grim authority of the computer. The results simply accentuate the traditional effects of piecework. People take shortcuts, skip safety measures, gobble sandwiches at their machines in place of lunch, panic when their machines break, squabble with others over equipment and assignments, develop the symptoms of stress and anxiety, go on medication, yearn for a return to hourly wages. Nor is the garment industry unique. Computerized piecework is taking shape in office work, communications, retailing. Output per worker is easily tabulated at a telephone switchboard, and no bundling or ticketing is required.

22 Speed-up can be implemented by a directive on the screen instead of a hectoring forelady. Some supermarket checkout counters already tally piecework. Even homework is reappearing, via portable terminals and screens.

Canada Day and Chinese New Year Celebrations, 1983
Chinese Canadian National Council

This is hardly the placid, humming, technologically sophisticated future usually envisioned for us by the prophets of hi-tech. By picturing a work-world largely without people, they manage to gloss over the human costs technological change brings with it. On Spadina, in the *shmatah* business, the human beings are unavoidable, before and after technological change. Perhaps today's garment industry evokes so much hostility not because it's a relic of the past, but as a harbinger of the future — one in which working people will be forced to continue their battle to maintain their dignity, much as they always have.

At any rate, not everyone has given up on industrial Spadina. Toronto's city council and the various industry players have plans for a "facelift" of the street, plus daycare, health care, English-language training, a half-million-square-foot Fashion Mart and fashion information kiosks. Kiosks! Perhaps it's not time for nostalgia yet. I take a last look down industrial Spadina — what's left of it — then turn and cross Dundas.

From here up to College has always been the retail/commercial part of Spadina. Perhaps we should add "cultural." I stand under the marquee of the Victory theatre. Whoops — not the Victory — the Golden Harvest. This theatre has known many incarnations. It used to be the Standard, a Yiddish theatre, and political-cultural projects like *Eight Men Speak* went on its stage. In the mid-1930's it became the Strand, a movie house. After the Second World War it was renamed, naturally, the Victory and became a burlesque house. When I was growing up it was a centrepiece of adolescence. Since we lacked any comparison, the strip shows seemed like the real thing. We didn't know how prissy they were, in the Toronto way. G-strings and pasties were obligatory; numerous rules restrained the performances of the talent. Since 1975 it has been a Chinese theatre. In fact, the whole area has become a sort of Chinese theatre.

Hanging Out, Dundas and Spadina, April, 1985
Pamela Gawn

This January, for instance, during Chinese New Year's celebrations at this corner, a massive, multi-coloured paper lion's head was suddenly confronted by a much starker and darker lion's head carried by black-clad youth. Rain was pouring down. The two met head-on and tensely circled each other. The police on duty fingered their nightsticks. Some people said it represented a conflict between Chinese and Vietnamese; others said it was part of the ceremony.

Spadina has become about as Chinese as it once was Jewish. The new community stretches east along Dundas to the original Chinatown, south to include the grandiose China Court at Sullivan — in all directions. It differs from Jewish Spadina. The Chinese who came in the recent wave from Hong Kong brought a great deal of capital with them. They're the richest immigrants ever to enter Canada. Ethnicity no longer plays a controversial role. Half a century ago immigrants were considered dangerous revolutionaries. It was a crime to speak publicly in a

23

foreign language. Today multiculturalism is about as controversial as Motherhood — probably less if you think about some issues raised by the Women's Movement. Every political party courts the ethnic vote. And each June Toronto gets Caravan — two weeks of ethnic pavilions serving Kielbasa and curry to tourists from suburbia with special "passports" to downtown.

Similarities persist, though. Chinese women are a big part of the workforce in Spadina's garment factories. Chinese families avidly pursue success; the second generation streams into the universities. And the Chinese community did choose Spadina as its home. *Plus ça change* — however that goes in Yiddish or Chinese. That's the kind of street it is.

Spadina and Dundas has always been a great hanging-around corner. Buying newspapers, swapping stories, arguing politics (if you got involved you'd go for a corned beef sandwich or a plate of blintzes and carry on battling). A few steps north, past the liquor store, I glance at the hoardings over the old site of Shopsy's. It still lives, still vibrates with life and food, but miles from here, on Front Street across from the O'Keefe Centre. And it still sees many of its old customers, but now they drop in after the touring version of *Evita*, or the National Ballet. Directly opposite, the other deli, Switzer's, still serves pastrami and new dills (when they're in), though in another way both establishments are gone, sold to corporate entities by the families who began them. Shopsy's has even become a brand at supermarket meat counters in *Judenrein* shopping plazas throughout Canada — it's owned by Lever Brothers!

But here's an eatery still tied to its roots — United Bakers Dairy restaurant — run with warmth and taste by the Ladovskys. Through the window I can see Herman, the aging elf, son of the original United Baker. The last time I had a plate of his vegetarian chopped liver, he waved a copy of my letter to the editor of the *Canadian Jewish News* at me. "So you're still giving it to them!" he said, patting me on the back. His son Phil is beside him. Phil used to take kids on canoe trips in Temagami during the summers. He plays jazz piano when he's not behind the cash.

A little beyond, at the corner of St. Andrew's, is the Labor Lyceum. It doesn't look like a Labor Lyceum now. A Chinese pagoda, maybe, but the Chinese restaurant that took it over has closed, too. Now a new one is going up — Hong Kong's famous something or other. Even in the glory days of Jewish Spadina this was more than a union hall; it was a cultural locus. Emma Goldman lectured here. The renowned anarchist spoke often and brilliantly on themes like literature, drama (Ibsen) and liberated sexuality (or free love as they used to say with a sense of danger). I recently asked a Spadina old-timer if he had known her. "Who didn't?" he replied. "She died in my house." I must have looked sceptical. "It's in her book, *Living My Life*," he insisted, and I didn't think to ask how she'd covered her own death in her autobiography. "What was she like?" I asked. "She was a very unusual person," he said

Emancipation Day, Victoria Square, July, 1961
Wreath-laying ceremony by Frank Richardson and Wallace Pleasant, veterans of the First World War, at the memorial to the War of 1812.
Toronto Telegram, York University Archives (Box 344, 2294)

Aaron and Sarah Ladovsky, Rose Lieberman and Rose Green
United Bakers, 338 Spadina, 1920's
Ladovsky family

slowly. "She wanted what they want today — the women's liberation." A crony of his, an elderly woman, chimed, "Isn't that the way it always is. One generation fights so another generation will have." Emma spent several years in Toronto between the wars. She had an office on Spadina just above Queen, and she indeed died here in 1940. Her body lay in the Labor Lyceum for a memorial service. Then it was embalmed and sent to Chicago, where she was buried alongside the Haymarket martyrs.

This part of Spadina is jammed with knick-knack shops and storefront Chinese restaurants. Each restaurant has a sign — and sometimes a newspaper clipping to back it up — saying it serves the best Chinese food in Toronto, Canada or the Western World. I have tried many of these places and the claim is true. Across the street, at the corner of Baldwin (ah, Dr. Baldwin!) is the Paramount. It's a black bar that serves smelts and has live music. Its original version, a block south, was the Paramount Kosher Hotel.

For blacks Spadina was part of the District. Many of us who first found a Canadian home on Spadina were late-comers: Jews, Hungarians, Chinese, South Americans. Not blacks. They came here with the Loyalists. In 1799 there were fifteen blacks in York. In the 1850's there were one thousand blacks in a population of forty-eight thousand. There was a black landowner, a member of Parliament, an alderman. In Victoria Square, just west of Spadina near the oldest part of the street, is a memorial to "the Colored Corps and Indians who gave their lives in the war" — the War of 1812! There have been successive waves: escaped slaves on the Underground Railroad, blacks from the Maritimes, Caribbean blacks, recent American arrivals. They have continued to feel at home on Spadina.

On the west side of the street are some of the pioneers of Szechuan food for the non-Chinese restaurant-goer. Their spicy dumplings were a daring departure once, not to mention their hot and sour soup. Yesterday's revolutions become today's clichés.

At the corner of Cecil is Grossman's. Al Grossman and his family opened their kosher-style cafeteria on Spadina at exactly the wrong time — 1951 — just as Jews were starting their exodus from the area. By 1957 when Grossman's finally received its liquor licence (after opposition from various United Church ministers) there weren't many kosher-style diners left. Meanwhile the Hungarian Revolution had come and gone, and a flood of new immigrants were in Toronto. Many settled — surprise — around Spadina. Goulash appeared on the Avenue. The Grossman secret was adaptability-rooted, one surmises, in a tolerant nature and a good business sense. They brought in gypsy fiddlers and altered the menu. Over the years they made other changes: soul food, egg rolls — whatever the times required — and the appropriate music as well.

In the 1960's a new kind of generational immigrant — hippies — moved into the area. They were self-styled outcasts, internal migrants from sectors of Canadian society like suburbia and the middle classes. Many roomy man-

sions of former times turned into communes and co-ops. Hippies found their way to Grossman's. So did students from the University of Toronto, as the student population expanded. By mid-decade draft-dodgers from the United States — immigrants fleeing the war in Vietnam — had started constructing a new "American ghetto" on Spadina. When they said "before the War," they meant 1962. Their newspaper, *Amex*, was nearby. They hung out at Grossman's. Artists and musicians were migrating from The Pilot on Yonge Street. Behind the counter Al Grossman watched. In the front room bands played. In 1970 at Grossman's the first and only People's Poet award was conferred on Milton Acorn.

Milt is, in my opinion, our best poet, though I'd be partial to anyone who wrote no more than "I've tasted my blood too much/to love what I was born to." Especially if he also said, "I have called myself many things; but I guess the one that sticks is 'Revolutionary Poet' — that is revolutionary in the political sense, not the poetic sense."

Milt has gone back to Prince Edward Island now, but for years he lived in a room at the Waverley Hotel on Spadina just above College. He was not the simplest guy to get along with. Personally I was irked by his tendency to win arguments by inventing historical facts. The combination of his views, his talent and his personality did not result in an easy life. Almost any day you could see him walking into lamp posts on this section of Spadina. In 1969 he published a stupendous book, *I've Tasted My Blood*. It was a gift to his country. The year's Governor-General's award for poetry was divided between a dyspeptic volume of pseudo-American verse and a book by Milt's ex-wife! The lamp posts must have clanged that day. Furthermore, one of the judges was an out-and-out U.S. citizen! The response by poets, editors, readers, the government of Prince Edward Island, Milt's drinking partners and innumerable others was the People's Poet award ceremony, convened at Grossman's — the laureate-designate's favourite watering-hole and an easy stumble down from the Waverley. The poet himself contributed the thought, "You cannot buy my truth but you can buy my scorn." For a day Grossman's was the capital of Canadian nationalism, cultural division.

I continue up the street. *Guerrilla*, Toronto's alternate newspaper in the sixties and seventies, had its office somewhere around here. Across the street is Gwartzman's, where I buy the pens I use as I sit and write this account. Spadina seems to accommodate small family businesses — the places you'd rather go to even if they cost more. When the family sells — Shopsy's, Switzer's, ten years ago Grossman's, too — the name stays and, less often, the feeling.

There's the Elmo, the El Mocambo, one of the first restaurants in Toronto to get a liquor licence, in 1948. The neon palm tree continued to glitter on the sign even after the place changed hands and became a centre for pop and rock. Local bands downstairs, no cover. International hotshots and the odd Canadian above. It had its fifteen

No Music from the Bar

No music from the bar. Damn Sunday
When no stripper wags her miscellaneous
*   cuts*
Of long pig, grotesquely meaning to look
*   horney;*
No singer whines impressions of a Yank
*   in a rut*
Dripping polluted tears for damn dead
*   Dixie:*
Or Continentalist band beats and blares
You deaf, for what's meant to be eternity.

Idiotic noise, transmogrified to music
Or something like that, in my muffled
*   room upstairs*
Blurred me til I slept like a mosquito
Insentient to the worse civic bedlam —
Not quite serene: But now, fixed to this
*   bed of fright*
Through churning Sunday night in the
*   volcano*
Of a cannonading city; I'm frigged —
With no note to play against metallic
*   discord*
Short of getting up and making rage my
*   lord ...*
Sleepless in Toronto — home of the
*   homesick.*

Jackpine Sonnets, Milton Acorn,
Steel Rail Press, 1977

Gwartzman's Art Supplies, 448 Spadina, 1985
Elizabeth Feryn

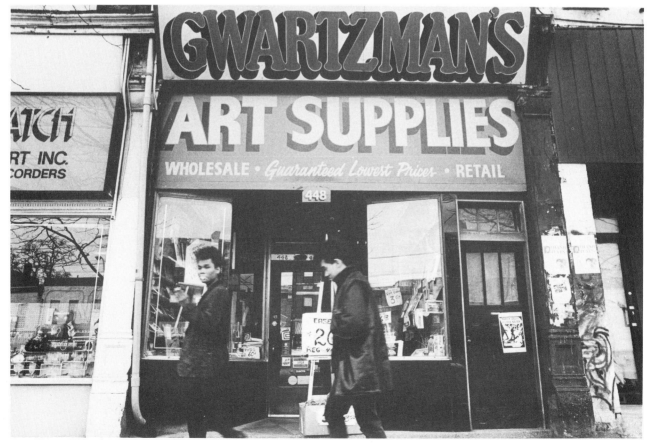

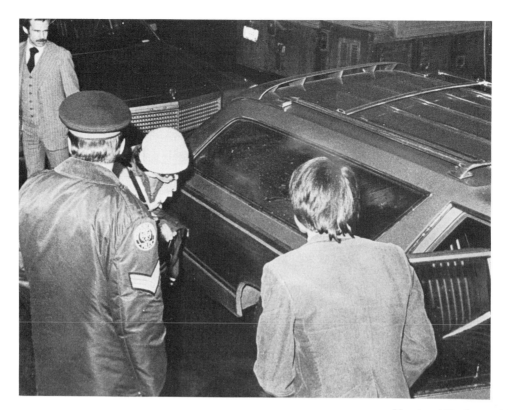

seconds of fame in 1977 when Margaret Trudeau attended
a Rolling Stones concert there. Its owner isn't really a
rock fan. "I like jazz but jazz fans don't drink," he says.
I understand it's up for sale.

Just past the Elmo is the Crest (once the Crescent) Grill.
A good place for breakfast if you're not a seven-year-old
going to summer camp for the first time. Kitty-corner on
the north side of College is Tip Top Tailors — a legend in
the Canadian garment industry. Tip Top got its break with
army contracts back in the *First* World War. They say
somebody knew somebody who knew Sam Hughes, the
lunatic minister of war at the time. Now Tip Top is part of
the huge Dylex corporation.

Just behind Tip Top is the Clarke Institute of Psychiatry, where my mother has been a secretary for twenty
years. Before that Dad didn't want her to work because it
would reflect on him as breadwinner. Funny, now he
doesn't work anymore but she does — and right on Spadina. Beside it is the Addiction Research Foundation, where
my brother had a job until he and his family went to
Saskatchewan. He says he wants to return to Toronto
now. I wonder if he'll end up back on Spadina. In the
1960's he had a little apartment over a store down the
street where he ate a lot of brown rice. This walk is getting sticky again: that feeling of every stream in life
tumbling into one channel called Spadina.

On the west side attached to the Waverley is the Silver
Dollar, a raunchy bar. Murray McLauchlan was precise
when he sang, "I went to the Silver Dollar/ Looked a
stranger in the eye." Just north is the Scott Mission. I was
intrigued as a kid when I went by and saw the lineup of
destitute men waiting for a meal or a bed. Why intrigued?
I guess I became aware that there was a part of reality
nearby that was different from the secure world I
inhabited. The Scott Institute began in the early years of
the century as a Protestant mission to Toronto's Jews. Its
director was the Reverend Morris Zeidman, who had been

28

a teenage Jewish convert. During the Depression he concentrated less on conversion than on social relief, which led to a split with his sponsors. In 1948 he moved to the current location and changed the name. The Mission still serves hundreds of thousands of meals a year, along with some religion.

I'm at the Crescent. Benjamin's, the Jewish funeral home, used to be just around the corner. That was where we buried Grandpa, who struck Eaton's in 1911, after he dropped at my feet from a heart attack during the seder at Aunt Betty's exactly twenty years ago last Passover. I didn't feel badly for him. It was the only night of the year he knew he would be with all the members of his family. He must have chosen it. Since then Benjamin's has moved north to Steeles Avenue. Its place on Spadina has been taken by the Far East funeral chapel.

Once you're north of the Crescent, the air seems thinner. Or maybe it's the atmosphere. The street is just as wide (it doesn't narrow until Bloor), but something is lacking. Still, even where Spadina attenuates in space or time, it retains its kick.

Stop Spadina Leaflet, 1969-70
Stop Spadina Collection, York University Archives

D.D.T.
Thalidamide.
Phosphates.
Cyclamates.
Carbon monoxide.
Expressways.

Sometimes progress can be deadly. It usually happens when men are so passionately trying to solve one problem that they inadvertently create others.
We've learned.
But only after the damage was done.

A lot of people are worried that the Spadina Expressway will be one of those hasty mistakes.
No one knows really what it will cost. Several politicians and construction companies told us 70 million dollars. Now, they say 200 million. Or more.

No one knows for sure how much extra we'll pay in taxes.

Or what's going to happen to the displaced people who are unfortunate enough to be living in the expressway's path.
Or what's to be done about the parks and ravines that will be destroyed. What about the air pollution Spadina will bring.
And the noise.
Or how rapid transit might help.

The point is, right now there are a lot of questions. And very few answers.
If you have doubts, give help, support (even money) to "Stop Spadina", 373 Huron St. T.O. 181. Phone 964-8162
For once, let's get the answers, first.

The Spadina Expressway.
Do we really know what we're doing.

Antifibre e l'estate 1983

Touring the Garment District, 1982
From left: alderman John Sewell, designer Alfred Sung, MPP Dan Heap.
Olivia Chow

Fifteen years ago this part of the Avenue — below Bloor — was the beachhead for an attack called the Spadina Expressway, a concrete and asphalt assault weapon aimed at the heart of downtown. It was designed to load up with thousands of cars in the suburbs, hurtle them toward the city, faster and thicker the closer they came; then spew them like buckshot when they hit the Avenue — shattering neighbourhoods, slashing rights-of-way, killing the garment district and thousands of jobs, spreading pollution. The project based itself on the private ethic of the automobile; it was the antithesis of Spadina with its streetcar tracks, busses and all those *people* in the street. It pitted the suburbs against Spadina. They were the new face of old Toronto. The Family Compact still lived in Rosedale, but spoke through the voices of North York and the Metro Council. The expressway was declared inevitable, like all new weapons systems. It was Progress.

Stop Spadina was the cry of resistance; it might as well have been Save Spadina. Businessmen on the Avenue organized. Homeowners in the Annex nearby joined to protect their neighbourhoods (and/or property values, which soared in the aftermath). The movement was the training-ground for a generation of civic reformers who went on to battle developers. They received support from far beyond the Spadina community itself, probably because they were fighting for a community — a place in which people live, work, walk and talk. Even those who

30

had moved away still recalled, perhaps nostalgically, that quality of community which no longer existed in their lives. They didn't miss the poverty but they missed the rest. To perhaps universal amazement, the protest succeeded. The weapons system was not deployed. Progress stopped at Eglinton Avenue.

It wasn't thousands of needle-trade workers chanting in Yiddish and relating local issues to the international socialist struggle. In fact, the shock troops were often middle-class renovators from the tree-lined streets north of Bloor. But it was Spadina-esque anyway. And it had the old Indian name.

In 1981 it happened again. The unexceptional member of Parliament for Spadina was despatched to the Senate. The Trudeau government was clearing a seat for Liberal hustler and kingmaker Jim Coutts. The plot was simple: Coutts would occupy the seat in a by-election, step into the cabinet and possibly run for the leadership following Trudeau's expected resignation. Spadina was a neat fit. It had been Liberal federally since the days of (Senator) David Croll. Its numerous ethnic communities had been loyal to the party many times over.

The opposition parties wearily sent their candidates into this ambush. The NDP nominated Dan Heap, who had carried the party banner through many a losing fight. The voters of Spadina elected him by a narrow margin. Or perhaps they rejected Coutts. Or just declined to play their assigned role.

Undaunted, Coutts set up an office and spent three years acting as *if* he was the member for Spadina. He did favours, he fixed things in Ottawa. You couldn't go anywhere in the riding and not find him. In 1984 he bounded up to my door about an hour after the federal election had been announced. This campaign made his last effort look casual. Trudeau came to the riding. Other cabinet ministers came. Coutts gave picnics and parties. He was sprightly, he looked like he'd just stepped from the shower. Dan Heap and his canvassers shlepped forlornly from door to door. Poor Dan — at least he'd been to Ottawa once.

This time Heap won soundly. He and his wife were, let us say, unglamorous. He was a stolid, Anglican-ordained

Fitness Class, Jewish Community Centre, April, 1985
Lorne Fromer

worker-priest with a pedestrian speaking style. J.B. Salsberg he was not. But Spadina was still Spadina. It wouldn't play its part. It didn't go along.

At the very top of this stretch, where Spadina Avenue ends at Bloor, stands the old Y, now the Jewish Community Centre. I still think of it as the new Y. When it opened in 1954 I joined. I was twelve and we'd moved from downtown into Forest Hill Village, but I'd ride my CCM bike down to shoot baskets, swim or bounce on the wondrous trampoline. A few years ago I joined for the second time; I even became a member of the Health Club (*two* towels plus sauna). But I found my fellow members discussed their health as though they'd just made a deal. ("I got my pulse rate down to sixty. How about that? That's eight points in two weeks. Whadda *you* got?") The fitness classes were like singles' parties and everyone was already fit anyway. My membership lapsed again.

I'm driving up Spadina. In the car with me is a twelve-year-old. She's just finished her Saturday afternoon drama class. We're passing a block and a half north of Dundas, between D'Arcy and Baldwin, where I used to visit my grandparents on high holidays at the Hebrew Men of England synagogue — the *Londoner shul*. I savour Spadina. "What do you think of this street?" I ask her. "I hate it," she says. I swallow my composure and ask why. "It's ugly and it's messy and the cars all park in the wrong direction," she says flatly, listing many things I like about Spadina. We drive in silence and I turn off at College.

She's from Kingston, the heartland of Upper Canadian Toryism. She has relatives in Rosedale and spends her summers on a farm. Like many kids of her generation she's had a confused, sometimes chaotic family life. She senses the messiness of adolescence just ahead. She'd like

Saturdays at Suzy's, 154 Spadina, April, 1985
Elizabeth Feryn

32

things to be clear and unequivocal. She has no need for any trendy, artificial, vicarious mayhem, thank you.

Still, I'd like to think Spadina can serve her. Maybe some time in the turbulent period she's just about to enter, or on the other side of it, she'll think about the street and say, "Well, at least it was different. So things can be different. And if they can be different, maybe they should be different..."

I guess for me Spadina is an alternative. That's the reaction it evokes in me, the relationship I have to it. An alternative is all that's required to undermine the *status quo*. Undermine, not overthrow. But on the rigid grid of Toronto's streets, and the rigid grid of values and attitudes in much of Canadian life, I'm glad to be able to take a route that doesn't go along.

On the other hand, maybe she'll always hate Spadina. After all, everyone takes her own walk down the Avenue. Because that's the kind of street it is...

Spadina is an anomaly and a symbol — slightly
overscaled, yet unprepossessing and resonant
with a dense and particular history.

Most of the history is unwritten. It survives
in fragments of colourful stories and lingering
memories, in photographs and in its neighbour-
hoods. In reconstructing Spadina's past, we
draw upon these scattered and incomplete re-
sources to assemble a composite picture — to
connect the collective memories to the present
realities. The unifying element throughout
Spadina's complex history has been the physical
street itself — the site.

"The Avenue" is the main street for the local
industrial and residential neighbourhoods —
"the District." Within the city's economy,
Spadina produces materials and goods in the
industrial sector with the factories, distributors
and wholesalers of the garment district, and a
wide range of services with its stores, res-
taurants and bars. The street has also become
an enclave for artists, musicians and street
people who co-exist on the fringe of the city's
economy. Throughout the years it has been this
combination of industrial activity and cultural
street life that has established Spadina's reputa-
tion as a cultural and political pressure point.

More than any other nineteenth-century Tor-
onto street, Spadina's destiny has been deter-
mined by its scale and width. The combination
of nineteenth-century residential and commer-
cial street-wall with early twentieth-century

industrial loft buildings has enabled it to maintain an architectural integrity. Yet the street has adapted both physically and imaginatively to the 1980's, incorporating layers of its past into its present circumstances.

But Spadina's flexibility and width may also be its doom. With the ongoing Spadina Expressway controversy to the present debate over the domed stadium and the railway lands development, the street is under constant threat of being turned into an auto route for those on their way to somewhere else, or a dumping ground for parked cars, as the city redevours and redevelops itself.

In reconstructing Spadina's past, this book draws upon historical and contemporary photographs — from institutions, unions, the media, private collections and independent photographers. These pictures are juxtaposed with the individual stories and historical documents to form a composite image, but not a definitive one. For Spadina has never been a single homogeneous community; its history is a complex layering of cultures, ideas and historic confrontations.

The photographs and panoramas of both sides of the Avenue are organized geographically, starting at the lake and proceeding north to Spadina Crescent and Bloor Street with the gradual elevation of the land from the lake "ishtadinauh."

Foot of Brock Street (Spadina), c. 1862
The men on the right are moving log booms in the harbour as Great Lakes sailing ships dock at the Northern Elevator wharf.
From *A Toronto Album: Glimpses of the City That Was*, Mike Filey, University of Toronto Press, 1970

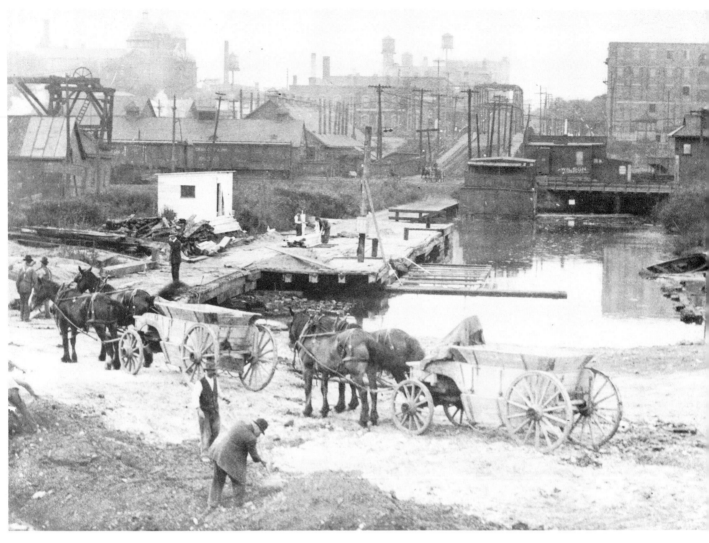

Spadina Wharf, c. 1909
Looking north. Loretto Abbey on Wellington Street is on the far left. The wagons in the foreground are dumping waste fill into the lake.
William James, City of Toronto Archives (235)

Foot of Spadina, c. 1907
Looking south from the original Spadina Bridge. The Northern Elevator is in the distance.
Baldwin Room, Metro Reference Library (T 30204)

**Workers Constructing
Spadina Sewer, April,
1919**
Public works photograph,
Toronto Harbour Commission,
Public Archives Canada (PA
96843)

The Northern Elevator

The first grain elevator at the foot of Brock
Street (Spadina Avenue) was erected in 1870 by
the Northern Railway Company. Built on a pier
extending into the lake, it had a storage capacity
of 260,000 bushels and was 140 feet high. It was
destroyed by fire in November, 1908.

In association with the redevelopment of the
Spadina railyards in the 1920's, Toronto Elevators Ltd. constructed a massive 2 million-bushel
elevator at the foot of Peter Street. In 1983 the
Toronto Terminal Elevator was demolished. The
development of the St. Lawrence Seaway and
the change in grain-handling methods had made
the elevator obsolete, and it stood in the way of
redevelopment plans for the waterfront.

The Spadina Railyards

The Spadina Railyards were located at the foot of Front Street on land set aside for a public promenade on the lakeshore — the Esplanade. The depot for the Northern Railway (originally the Toronto, Simcoe & Huron Railway) was on the west side of Brock Street (Spadina) and its main line went north over the historic portage route to Georgian Bay. A "Great Railway Festival" was held in December, 1855, at the new Northern Railway workshops at the foot of Brock Street to celebrate the completion of the Toronto-Hamilton rail link.

The Grand Trunk Railway, under the skilful

management of Casimir Gzowski, built its railyards on the east side of Brock Street in 1857. The original railyards included a machine shop and an unusual domed roundhouse.

In the nineteenth century many railway workers lived on Spadina in order to be within walking distance of work.

The Northern Railway buildings were taken over by the Grand Trunk in 1888 and merged into the Canadian National Railway in 1923. The CNR Spadina Railyards were extensively redeveloped in 1927-28 at the same time as the Spadina Bridge was extended and rebuilt. The major

feature of the yards was the Roundhouse where locomotives were serviced and cleaned. It was composed of 36 stalls with a twin-span type turntable and was approached by 50 tracks.

The Spadina Railyards are now being demolished to make way for massive rail lands redevelopment. The only remaining element of the yards will be the CPR Roundhouse to the east of Peter Street, which is to be retained as a railway museum. The development of the rail lands and Harbourfront will greatly affect the transit, industrial and residential uses of southern Spadina Avenue in coming years.

Spadina Bridge Under Construction, November, 1925, to June, 1926

Top, from left: John Boyd, Public Archives Canada (PA 87256); City of Toronto Archives (VIA 27); City of Toronto Archives (VIA 75) *Bottom, from left:* City of Toronto Archives (VIA 39); John Boyd, Public Archives Canada (PA 87445); Toronto Transit Commission (4903)

Northern Railway Offices 4-6 *Spadina*

The first brick building on the northwest corner of Front and Spadina was the Northern Railway office. It was close to the Northern Railway station at the foot of Brock (Spadina), which was the terminus for the Collingwood/Georgian Bay and the Huntsville/Muskoka rail lines. The terminus was closed after the amalgamation of passenger terminals at Union Station.

The two-storey square, Georgian-style building was remarkable for its surface detail and patterned brickwork.

During the early 1900's the building served as the headquarters for the British Welcome League, which assisted newly arrived immigrants, and as an office of the YMCA. An auto accessories shop took the building over in the 1920's and subsequently demolished it.

The present building on the site, a one-storey garage, operates as an auto-body shop and car rental outlet.

Northern Railway Offices, c. 1860
Anonymous watercolour, Baldwin Room, Metro Reference Library (T 12336)

Laying Streetcar Tracks, Front and Spadina, June, 1926
Looking north. The Northern Railway offices are on the left.
Public works photograph, City of Toronto Archives (VIA 56)

**Rainy Day, Front Street,
October, 1926**
Looking east from Spadina.
Transit record photograph,
Public Archives Canada
(PA 54332)

Clarence Square

Clarence Square first appears in an 1834 map by
R.H. Bonnycastle, as part of the redistribution of
the garrison reserve surrounding Fort York. The
square forms the eastern end of Wellington
Place with Victoria Square on the western end.
It was originally designed to be part of the
public promenade along the waterfront. The
Georgian terraced houses that surround the
square on the north side were built in the late
1870's. These were renovated in 1968 and many
now serve as offices and apartments.

Summer Reading, Clarence Square, c. 1970
Yuri Humphrey

Spadina Avenue, June, 1949
Looking north from Clarence Square on the right, before the widening of Spadina from King to Front.
Public works photograph, City of Toronto Archives (RDY 1947)

Clarence Square, October, 1913
Looking east to Spadina. The Darling Building is on the right.
City of Toronto Archives (Parks 198)

43

Farewell Party, Loretto Alumni Association, Loretto Abbey, June, 1927
The first house on the site between Front and Wellington was briefly the home of Anna Jameson. In 1867, the Sisters of Loretto bought the property and opened it as a boarding school and mother house. An extensive addition and a Baroque-style chapel were added in 1897. From 1930 until 1961 the buildings were used as a Jesuit seminary. A new building was erected on the site in 1963 by the Toronto *Telegram* and became the Toronto *Star* printing plant in 1971. In 1974 the *Globe & Mail* took over the building. The original revolving doorway from the Globe building at 140 King Street was added to the front lobby on Front Street, and the Wellington Street side became a parking lot.
Panoramic Camera Co., Merrilees Collection, Ontario Archives (Box 2, 152)

44

ONTO JUNE 25-26 1927

Toronto Negro Band, July, 1961
Wellington Place, looking east. Emancipation Day parade en route to Victoria Square.
Toronto Telegram, York University Archives (Box 344, 2294)

50   60   64   66

The Mexican Revolution

In 1911 Mexico was swept by a peasant and pro-letarian revolution. The ideas that fed the popular struggle were probably developed in Toronto.

In 1906 leaders of Mexico's opposition movement took refuge in the U.S., forming the Mexican Liberal Party (PLM), a political-military organization which eventually overthrew the dictator Porfirio Diáz.

Ricardo Flores Magón (an anarchist lawyer, editor and president of the PLM), his brother Enrique (PLM treasurer) and their colleague Juan Sarabia (PLM secretary) sought safety in Canada from March until the end of August, 1906. Diáz offered a $20,000 reward for Ricardo's capture, and Pinkerton's and Furlong's private police scoured the U.S. and Canada for the radical leaders. There is evidence that the men lived on Spadina during their exile. They masqueraded as Italians, working in construction.

While in Toronto, PLM leaders remained in constant mail contact with colleagues in exile in St. Louis, Missouri, and drafted the manifesto and program of their party. On July 1, 1906, it was published in the newspaper, *Regeneración*, in an edition of 750,000 copies. They called for the eight-hour day, universal public education to age fourteen, health and safety improvements in factories and mines, workmen's compensation, land to the peasants and protection of Mexico's indigenous peoples. Their program was the major intellectual stimulus for the 1911 revolt. The PLM leaders received support from American socialists and anarchist groups and from the IWW (Industrial Workers of the World). The major points of their program were written into the Mexican constitution of 1917, still in force today.

Juan Sarabia, Ricardo and Enrique Flores Magón, Authors of the PLM Manifesto

From *Obreros Somos...expressiones de la cultura obrera*, Museo nacional de Culturas populares, Mexico City

Regeneración, órgano de difusión del Partido Liberal Mexicano.

46

57

**Traffic on Spadina,
August, 1974**
Looking north from Front
during the 1974 Toronto
Transit strike.
James Lewcun, Globe & Mail

Warwick Bros. & Rutter Ltd. *57-59 Spadina*

Built in the early 1900's, the building that fronted on both King and Spadina had a floor space of over 55,000 square feet. It became the home of Warwick Bros. & Rutter, printers, publishers, bookbinders and stationers. The company was originally established in 1848; by 1911 it had a staff of three hundred. The site is presently occupied by Winners, a cut-rate chain retail outlet.

Russian Broadtail Coat, 1946
Norman Rogul Furs, 433 King at Spadina

Atlantic Fur Company, 431 King at Spadina, 1941
Toronto Jewish Congress Archives (24)

Warwick Bros. & Rutter, c. 1906
The printing plant was built on the southeast corner of King and Spadina around the Power House Hotel.
From *Toronto the Prosperous: 1872-1906*, Mail & Empire, Baldwin Room, Metro Reference Library

Power House Hotel, King and Spadina, c. 1900
The chambermaid in the third-floor window appears to be watching the photographer take the picture.
J.V. Salmon, City of Toronto Archives (1133)

Spadina Hotel at Night, 1979
Peter MacCallum

Spadina Hotel *484 King at Spadina*

The northwest corner lot at King and Spadina was bought by Samuel Richardson in 1873. On it he built a single frame house. In 1875 a larger three-storey building was erected and opened as Richardson House, a guest house and tavern. In 1883 a four-storey brick addition was added, with a second four-storey addition in 1887.

In 1906 the hotel was renamed the Hotel Falconer, and for a brief period in the 1910's it was known as Ziegler's Hotel. In 1917 it became the Spadina Hotel.

The second-floor front was redecorated in a tropical motif during the 1950's and was named the Cabana Room. The downstairs dining room was recently restored to its original 1883 decor, with Canadian chestnut and walnut wainscotting, chestnut window casings with shell glass

and high, curved ceilings with decorative mouldings.

The Cabana Room, under the management of Dan Poulos in the early 1980's, became one of the city's centres of local avant-garde music and art. Bands such as the Government, Mama Quilla II, the Honolulu Heartbreakers, the Hummer Sisters, as well as a number of performance artists such as Colin Campbell, Margaret Dragu, Andrew Patterson and Marion Lewis, have performed there in the past few years.

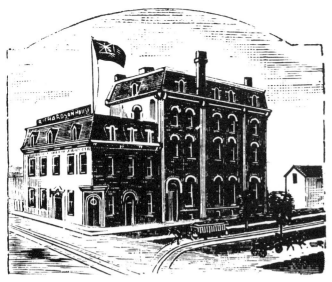

RICHARDSON HOUSE

COR. KING & SPADINA AVE.,
TORONTO.

THE MOST HANDSOME THOROUGHFARE IN THE DOMINION

The above house is heated by hot water, with all the modern improvements. Gas in every room. and for comfort is equal to any $2.00 per day house in Canada.

Terms $1.50 per day. Reductions to weekly boarders.

S. RICHARDSON. PROPR.

Richardson House, 1885
Advertising illustration from the Toronto Directory

Spadina Hotel, February, 1954
Baldwin Room, Metro Reference Library (S1-197)

Hotel Falconer, c. 1911
From *Greater Toronto and the Men Who Made It*, Baldwin Room, Metro Reference Library

80-82

**Spadina Hotel and the CN
Tower, April, 1985**
Elizabeth Feryn

**Untitled Installation by
Walter Gramming, 1983**
Cross-Ot, a German-
Canadian exchange exhibi-
tion held on the 4th floor of
80 Spadina, co-sponsored by
Chromozone, 320 Spadina,
and YYZ, 116 Spadina
Peter MacCallum

53

96   100   102   106-110   116-124

**Repaving After the
Removal of the Boulevard,
August 17, 1928**
Looking south from Adel-
aide, with the Spadina
Hotel on the right.
Public works photograph, City
of Toronto Archives (RDY 1203)

The Boulevard, July 13, 1928
Looking north from King, with the Spadina Hotel on the left. This photograph was taken before the widening of the street and the elimination of the treed boulevard that extended to Queen Street.
Toronto Transit Commission Archives (5986)

ILGWU Picket, Jac-An Junior, 1964
Balfour Building, 119 Spadina.
International Ladies Garment Workers Union

Adelaide and Spadina

"Most of the shops were on Adelaide and Spadina, the needle trades. Lunch time we used to go out to see other workers — talk to them. We had demonstrations when an election was on, when J.B. Salsberg was running, or Tim Buck. One hour for lunch — canvassing, leafletting, speakers on the corners.

I lived around where I worked. In those days, who had a car? We used to walk. You knew everybody. Once you had automobiles, people moved away. The woman stopped working in the trade, the husband could afford to make a living for both.

When you work in a factory, you become part of the factory. Your fellow workers are your friends, your family. When you went out on Spadina Avenue you saw everybody, talked to everybody. Even if you didn't work in the same shop, you still knew them from belonging to the union."

Interview with Sophie Mandel, May 27, 1984

Carrying Fur Pelts, 1970
Richmond at Spadina.
Marilyn Spink

123   121   119   105   101a   101

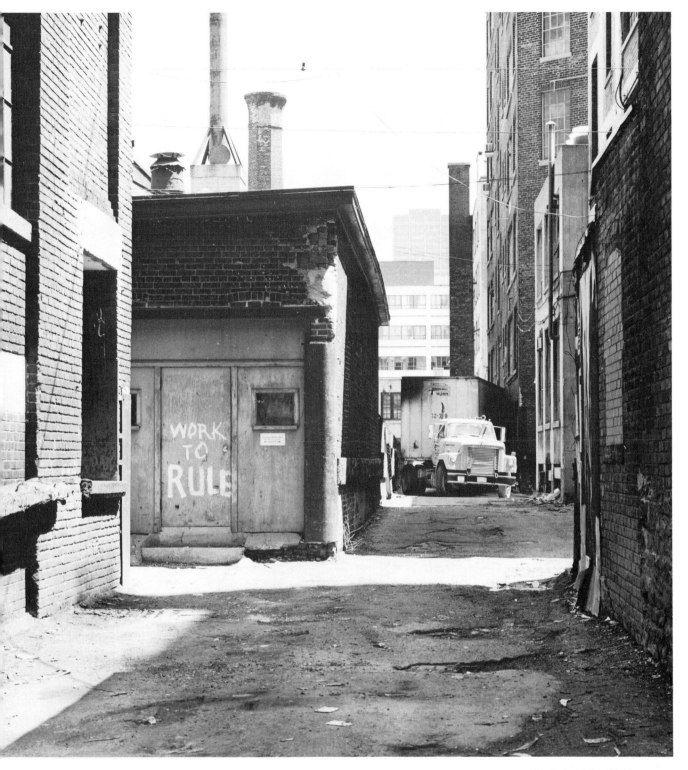

Work to Rule, 1984
Alleyway north of Richmond, east side of Spadina.
Peter MacCallum

57

Darling Building *104 Spadina*

This nine-storey warehouse and office building on the southwest corner of Adelaide and Spadina was completed in 1909. It was the first multi-storied loft building on Spadina, and one of the earliest cement buildings erected in the city. Built for Andrew Darling at a cost of $150,000, it housed his own company — the Darling Dress Company — and was identifiable by the large water tank on the roof.

The building still houses some of the major dress and coat manufacturing companies of Spadina Avenue.

58

Temperance Hall *144 Spadina*

This small building at the southwest corner of Richmond and Spadina was established by 1856 as the Temperance Hall, Sons of Coldstream Division. Known as the Baptist Mission, it was a meeting place for the Disciples of Jesus. It was known as "...a building much in need of repair but one in which the present writer believes that much earnest Christian work is done. He is acquainted with young women residing in the west end of our city, orphans, unbefriended, living on their daily labour, who have been much helped by the teaching given here in this little chapel." (*Toronto: Past and Present Until 1882*, P. Mulvany) The building continued as a Gospel Hall of the Plymouth Brethren until 1893.

In the early 1900's the site was occupied by a builder, Archer & Co., the Blundall Piano Co. and Dominion Foundry Supply. The building was demolished around this time. With the widening of Richmond Street and its connection to Balsam Street in the 1920's, Nat's Service Station, later Saul's Service Station, was built on an angle with the widened corner. The present two-storey building houses a ladies' garment retail outlet and a watch store.

96   100   102   106-110   116-124

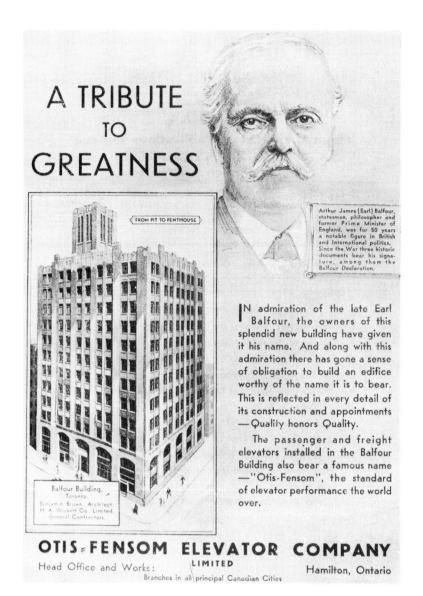

A Tribute to Greatness
From an advertisement in *Contract Record and Engineering Review*, October 22, 1930

Balfour Building *119 Spadina*
The present twelve-storey building on the northeast corner of Adelaide and Spadina was designed by Benjamin Brown in 1930. The loft building, with an art deco surface design and a fourteen-storey tower, forms the eastern gateway to Spadina Avenue.

The concrete and brick structure was built by H.A. Wickett Construction, with elevators by Otis-Fensom of Hamilton. The building was named in honour of the Earl of Balfour, a former British prime minister who, in the historic "Balfour Declaration" of 1917, committed the British government to support a Jewish homeland in Palestine.

Since the 1930's the Balfour Building has been one of the major garment industry buildings in the city.

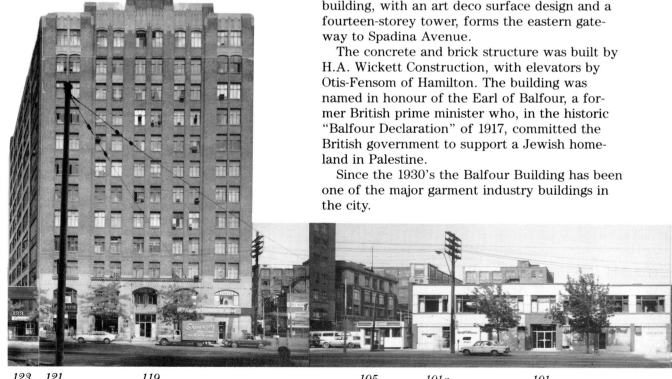

**Machine Operators, Mr.
Suli's Dress Factory, 1984**
Tenth floor, Balfour
Building.
Peter MacCallum

Balfour Building, c. 1931
Taken during construction
from the upper floors of the
Darling Building.
Toronto Jewish Congress
Archives (3308)

**Baby Clinic,
St. Christopher House,
September, 1914**
The St. Christopher Settlement House was established on Leonard Street (in the former mansion of Sir Casimir Gzowski) by the Presbyterian Church in 1912. It offered a range of social and athletic programs, was the site of the first Toronto daycare program and provided baby clinics which gave away pasteurized milk and formula to local mothers.
City of Toronto Archives (Health 334)

St. Andrew's Square Playground, August, 1914
Located at Richmond and Spadina, this was formerly the site of St. Andrew's Market. It is now a park and the location of a Metro public works garage.
City of Toronto Archives (Parks 425)

St. Andrew's Women's Basketball Champions, August, 1914
City of Toronto Archives (Parks 433)

Benjamin Brown, Architect

Benjamin Brown worked on Spadina Avenue during the industrial development of the street in the 1920's. Between 1920 and 1930 he designed nine buildings on the Avenue and a number of others in the vicinity: Standard Theatre, Dundas & Spadina, 1921; Empire Clothing Building, Phoebe & Spadina, 1926; Geller Brothers Garage, near St. Andrew's & Spadina, 1923; Reading Building, Camden & Spadina, 1925; Tower Building/Oxford Building, Adelaide & Spadina, 1927; Fashion Building, Camden & Spadina, 1929; Shiffer-Hillman Building, Phoebe & Spadina, 1929; Balfour Building, Adelaide & Spadina, 1930; Medico-Dental Building, College & Spadina, 1930. (Source: *Biographical Dictionary of Architects in Canada*, Robert Hill, editor, forthcoming)

The Tower Building *106-110 Spadina*

The present ten-storey loft building at the northwest corner of Adelaide and Spadina was erected by the Oxford Clothing Company, owned by the Poslun brothers and C. James. Usually known as the Tower Building, it was designed in 1927 by Benjamin Brown, who used a neo-Gothic motif on the exterior, focussing on the twelve-storey tower, and in the lobby interior.

The building was occupied mainly by ladies' apparel factories — cloaks, suits and dresses. One of the largest was the Superior Cloak Company, owned by the Posluns.

The Tower Building continues to be one of the major garment industry buildings on Spadina Avenue.

Casement Windows, Tower Building, July, 1984
Peter MacCallum

Lobby, Fashion Building, July, 1984
Peter MacCallum

106-110

116-124

Fashion Building, c. 1927
The final building differs
slightly in detail from the
architect's original drawing.
Toronto Jewish Congress
Archives (3307)

Fashion Building *130 Spadina*

For over thirty years William Coo operated a
grocery store at the northwest corner of Camden
and Spadina.

The present building was erected in 1925-27
by Goldberg Brothers and Hartman. The architect, Benjamin Brown, designed the eight-storey
building with neo-Gothic detail on the doorway
and upper floors. The small marbled lobby has
decorative patterns and plaster emblems inscribed with the word "Fashion."

The building continues to house some of the
major garment factories in Toronto.

130   136   140a   140   146   148

Time Clock, Fantasy Creations, 82 Spadina, 1981
Lorne Fromer

Wednesday on the Avenue

"One thing you must know. Toronto is strategically located within an area for places like Windsor, London, Kitchener, Chatham, Cambridge, Guelph, and then west — Hamilton of course, and to the north — Sudbury, the Sault, North Bay and Peterborough, and Kingston, Cornwall.

And on a Wednesday afternoon, none of the wholesalers on Spadina will allow you into their places. Because those people take a train and they get off at Union Station, they take a cab here to Spadina and Adelaide and they can do everything. I'm talking about retailers, regardless of what business they're in. They can hit thirty fur or dress manufacturers in one day. They don't have to travel from one end of the city to the other.

We have found that any furrier, other than a retailer, who opens in the suburbs, suffers. People who come in for the day do not want to travel way up north on Yonge Street, or to Mississauga. The people come in here on a Wednesday, boom!, they just buy whatever stock they need and then they hop on a train at 6 o'clock or 7 o'clock, and go home."

Interview with David Goodman, May 24, 1984

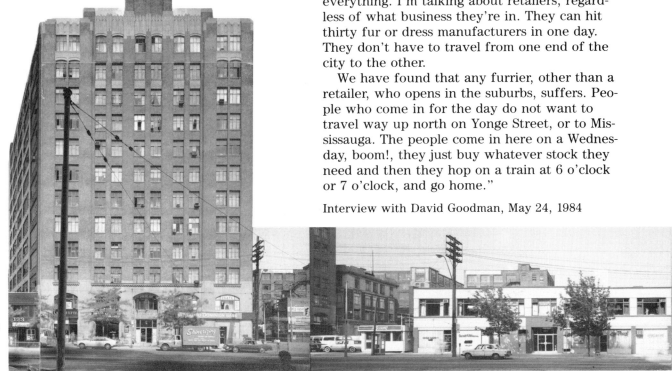

123   121   119   105   101a   101

Japanese

At the end of the Second World War, the Japanese-Canadians, or Nisei, were released from detention camps in western Canada and were officially dispersed across the country. "Toronto with its aura of big time glamour and job opportunities, was the most favoured destination. Japanese tramped the streets in a hunt for accommodations, enduring slammed doors and abusive rebuffs, their search likely ended in the Jewish section off Spadina Avenue, the core of the garment industry. Here the lodgers were often within walking distance of work, since the manufacturers and sundry firms owned by Jews were the least hesitant about hiring the unwanted. They were also the first willing to promote these employees to supervisory positions as well as to take on Nisei women in their offices, an unheard-of practice by non-Japanese West Coast businesses....But after several hundred had entered the city during the early stages of the eastward flow, it was declared off-limits. They could settle anywhere else in Ontario or Eastern Canada, even the townships and villages bordering Toronto, but only with the consent of the special Japanese Placement Officer could they live or work in the city proper." (*Nikkei Legacy, The Story of Japanese Canadians from Settlement to Today*, Toyo Takata, N.C. Press, Toronto, 1983)

Designers on Spadina, May, 1968
Counter-clockwise from the left front: model, Norman Rogul fox coat; model, JuniorVogue linen dress; Morris Hacker, presser, Primrose Garment Co.; Jerry Green, President, Green's Raw Furs Co.; Norman Rogul, President, Norman Rogul Furs; model, Ruth Dukas ballgown; Morris Watkin, President, Miss Sun Valley; Claire Haddad, Coty Award for Design, Claire Haddad Ltd.; Jack Klein, President, Sol Swartz Garments; model, David Rea wedding gown; Sam Sherkin, President, Sam Sherkin & Co.; David Rea, President, David Rea Dresses; David Weiser, Vice-president, Highland Queen Sportswear, designer of the Maple Leaf tartan; model, Claire Haddad award-winning negligee; Bernard Cowan, Vice-president, Ontario Fashion Institute; model, Sea Queen bikini; Murray Kates, President, Ontario Garment Salesmen's Market; Mary McInnis, fur consultant with Norman Rogul Furs.
Norman Rogul

67

Saturday Street Vendors near 154 Spadina, April, 1985
Elizabeth Feryn

Metromelt, Spadina south of Queen, December, 1977
The building on the right, with the art deco facade, was formerly St. Margaret's Church.
Barrie Davis, Globe and Mail
(77012-07)

130   136   140a   140

**City Sewer Worker, King
and Spadina, 1974**
Vincenzo Pietropaolo

Street Crowd, Camden and Spadina, 1950's
Kenny Collection, Fisher Rare Book Room, University of Toronto (Box 63, 179)

70

St. Margaret's Church, 161-163 Spadina, c. 1920
The church was converted into a factory in the late 1910's, and a yellow-brick art deco facade was added at a later date. The decorative buttresses, visible in the upper left of the photograph, can still be seen from Perry Lane. The building is now a factory and retail outlet.
William James, City of Toronto Archives (1735)

Toronto Joint Board, Amalgamated Clothing Workers of America, 1930's
The Amalgamated Clothing Workers Union was originally formed in Toronto in 1915 as a breakaway from the United Garment Workers, in order to better represent the interests of immigrant workers in the men's clothing industry.
Amalgamated Clothing Workers of America

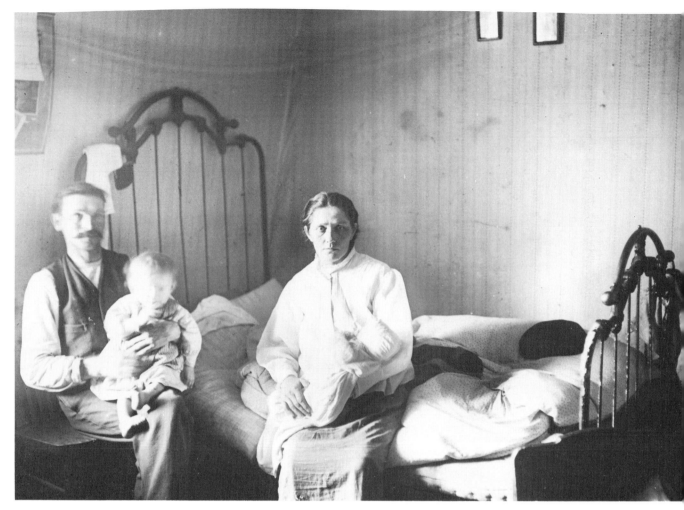

Anti-eviction Movement

"The Unemployed movement had its head-quarters at the United Church, the People's Church at Queen and Spadina. The Reverend Mr. McKay, he'd come with our delegations to City Hall when they'd cut people's water off or the electricity, or cut them off pogey. But McKay became too radical so they shipped him off to a mission somewhere.

When we'd hear about an eviction, we'd run off 500 or 1,000 leaflets in a hurry, turning the old crank on the mimeograph machine, and distribute them around the neighbourhood. In two hours we'd have 1,000 people around the house.

Immigrant Family, 152 Spadina, March, 1916
City of Toronto Archives
(Health 423)

We'd stop them from moving things out, but sometimes they'd bring in the Irish Constabulary, the backbone of the police force. They used to be rugged times."

Interview with Max Ilomaki, April, 1985.

130   136   140a   140

Children in Front of Church of All Nations, 1920's
Also known as Queen Street United Church, Queen and Spadina, demolished in 1984, now a vacant lot.
United Church Archives

146   148 150   152

Перший Укр. Нац. Роб Зїзд в Торонто 1930

Southeast Corner, Queen and Spadina

The building at the southeast corner of Spadina and Queen was originally an Odd Fellows Hall, designed by Langley and Burke. It was erected in 1888.

The corner store started as Devaney Brothers, a dry-goods merchant. Since the 1920's it has seen a succession of restaurants: the New Paris Cafe, Holm's Cafe & Quick Lunch, the Regal Sandwich Shop and most recently the Lite-Bite Restaurant. The second and third floors have had a variety of tenants over the years, from manufacturers to coal merchants. In the late 1930's it was a local political and trade union centre, with headquarters of the Workers Unity League and offices for various organizations: United Shoe Workers of America, Local 157; LaVoc Degli Italo-Canadesi; United Garment Workers Union; Brotherhood of Painters and Decorators, Local 864; United Brotherhood of Carpenters and Joiners, Local 1963; Upholsters and Furniture Workers Union, Local 149; Wreckers Local & International Hod Carriers Union; Window Cleaners Federal Union; Ontario Federation on Unemployment.

In 1984 Makos Furs undertook a major renovation of the building, restoring the original cupola and mouldings and opening a fur salon on the main floor.

Delegates, First National Ukrainian Workers Convention, 1930
M. Schlacter, Public Archives Canada (PA 1177 68)

74

Queen and Spadina, May, 1945
Looking east on Queen. The cars crossing the intersections are captured in motion by the slow shutter speed of the camera.
Toronto Transit Commission photograph, Public Archives Canada (PA 54010)

Communist Literature
Seized by police in the round-up of Communist Party officials in September, 1931, under Section 98 of the Criminal Code. The photograph was published in the November 10, 1931, Toronto *Telegram*.
Toronto Telegram York University Archives (Box 148, 1034)

Men's Public Lavatory,
Queen and Spadina,
c. 1900
The entrance to the
underground public lava-
tory was in the centre of
the boulevard south of
Queen. St. Margaret's
Church is on the right.
City engineer photograph,
Public Archives Canada (PA
55411)

Boulevard in Winter, 1901
Looking south from Queen and Spadina. The Darling Building is on the right and the entrance to the men's underground lavatory is in the foreground.
Public works photograph, City of Toronto Archives (7167)

Interior, Underground Public Lavatory, c. 1900
The sign on the closet doors reads: "Please do not use closets as urinals."
City engineer photograph, Public Archives of Canada (PA 55723)

Demolition of Turret, Bargain Benny's, 1972
The turret on the northwest corner corresponded to the cupola on the southeast corner of the Odd Fellow's Hall.
Peter MacCallum

160   162   166a   170   174

Pickford Theatre *382 Spadina*

Originally built as the Auditorium Theatre, one of the earliest movie houses in Toronto in the 1910's, the Mary Pickford Theatre is rumoured to have been owned at one time by Mary Pickford, the Toronto-born actress, and Douglas Fairbanks. The building's turret, together with the one on the southeast corner, marked the Queen and Spadina intersection.

Operated independently by C. Rotenberg during the 1930's, the theatre showed a variety of movies, from standard Hollywood fare to Soviet films. The third floor was the Leonard Athletic Centre, where local boxers like Sammy Luftspring got their start. As the Variety Theatre in the early 1950's, the building showed controversial American films such as "Salt of the Earth," which had been banned in the U.S. during the McCarthy period.

In the late 1950's the building was turned into a large bargain store called Benny's. Famous for its extravagant signs and wall paintings, and for its Scottie dog symbol, Benny's Pickfair Market extolled its wares to the street.

The building was demolished, along with its turret, in 1972, and the present two-storey brick building was erected.

Bargain Benny's Pickfair Close-out Mart, 1969-70
Yuri Humphrey

192   196-198   200   202

**Men at Work, Queen and
Spadina, May, 1922**
Toronto Transit Commission
Archives (TRANS 480)

The Old Leonard

"Oh, man, what a joint the old Leonard was in [1925]! It was located in a second floor loft, upstairs from the old Pickford Theatre at Queen and Spadina. The layout was one big room, with a boxing ring in the middle and chairs for about 150 ranged around it.

The place was filthy. It was grey with dust and dirt. The air was sharp with the stench of sweat mingled with cigar smoke. There was only one light, a great big white dazzler strung up over the centre of the ring, and the smoke of 150 cigars billowed through the light like a fog. ...All around me I could see the faces of these grown men set in fierce masks, the way fight fans can look when they imagine that it's really them up there, lashing out the punishment. ...

That night, the bout that these men had come to see was a real crowd-pleaser, featuring two Jewish boys, Harry Katz and Goody Rosen. An all-Jewish house couldn't lose. One of their own was bound to win. And in the end, it was Harry Katz who won ...

For Harry Katz, that night, with that audience, he was king. When he took the match the crowd roared, making an incredible explosion of noise in that tiny little room, deafening in my ears, but very, very exciting at the same time. Man, what a feeling of glory there was in that room. They presented him with this great big silver cup, and later, all the people who had been there waited down on the street for him, to cheer him again.

We waited too, my pa and I, and we became part of the procession going up Spadina, with everybody stopping and staring at us, and then cheering as Harry Katz led the parade, holding this great big silver cup in his arms.

He was a king, that's the only way I can describe it. A Jewish king who had won his crown with the force of his fists.

And I wanted so much to take his place that I could taste it."

Call me Sammy, Sammy Luftspring with Brian Swarbrick, Prentice-Hall, Scarborough, 1975.

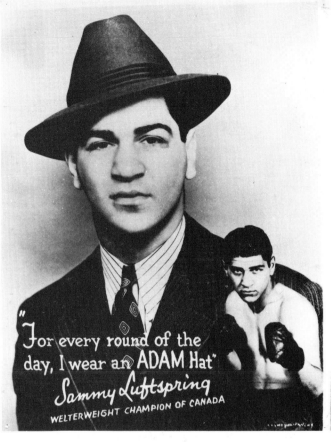

Sammy Luftspring, 1938
Sammy Luftspring, Norman (Baby) Yack, Dave Yack and Frank Genovese were Spadina-area children who became boxers. In 1936 Luftspring and Dave Yack were to represent Canada at the Munich Olympics. However, they joined the boycott of the Games, organized to protest Hitler's treatment of German Jews. They signed up for the alternative People's Olympics to be held in Barcelona, which were later cancelled due to the outbreak of the Spanish Civil War. Luftspring's professional boxing career was cut short when, as the reigning Canadian welterweight champion, he was blinded in a fight, one match away from the world lightweight title.
Toronto Jewish Congress Archives (2514)

169½   165

National Employment Office, 174 Spadina, c. 1954
Morning line-up to apply for unemployment insurance benefits and check job listings.
Canadian Tribune, Public Archives Canada (PA 93908)

Pedestrian, 1969
Looking north to 378 Queen, originally built as a branch of the Bank of Hamilton in 1902.
Yuri Humphrey

African Methodist Episcopal Church Conference, Soho and Queen, 1940's
Front row, from the left: Mrs. C.P. Jones,?, Rev. Wainer,?, Rev. C.P. Jones, Rev. Perry, Rev. John Holland, Bishop Gregg, Dr. Berry, Mrs. Ida Perry, Rev. Lord, Mrs. Vera Clarke, Mrs. Elizabeth Hackley, ?.

Second row: ?,?, Oliver Holland, Lloyd Perry, Alberta May Jones,?,?, Marie Hackley, Jocely Hackley (minister's wife), Mrs. Martha Stewart, Jeanette Woodcock, Grant Hackley,?,?,?,?. Third row: Geraldine Hackley, Mrs. Rachel Hackley, Mrs. Myrtle Hackley,?,?,?. Fourth row: Elaine Hackley, Mrs. May

Thomas,?, Mrs. Bonner (Oakville),?, Mrs. Maomi Pascoe, Mr. Coates (?). Fifth row: ?, Mr. Hiram Johnson.

Multicultural History Society, Ontario Archives (MSR 11515 #3)

192   196-198   200   202

Willison Square, late 1950's
Willison Square, off Spadina, was considered a slum area in the post-war period, and most of the housing was demolished to build the Alexandra Park housing development in 1966. The completed complex has 410 units and houses approximately 1,900 people.
CMHC, Public Archives Canada (PA 113399)

The Neighbourhood

"People who are not in the area think it's fascinating, but people who are don't think much of it. When you come up through it and you experience it, it's nice to read about it, but it's not nice to experience it. You have good moments, but you have more bad.

Sometimes you want to work and you can't work. The economics are bad and in those days it was certain jobs for certain people. The Jews had the garment industry, local blacks worked in service jobs — on the trains and as domestics. I guess if you were an Orangeman or something, you worked at City Hall.

The blacks didn't hang out together. The contact I had with other blacks would only be through the United Negro Improvement Association Hall or the church. They would have special clubs in an area like that, like West Indian clubs, social things, but it would be a loose type of thing. People would join because they're black.

Around Queen and Bathurst, when I was a kid, everyone was Ukrainian, Jewish, Hungarian, Polish. There was a great mix of eastern Europeans. And up further, you ran into a lot of Italians. The kids you hung out with, usually their mother could never speak English. You never really spoke correct English to them, you spoke a kind of funny English. That's all they seemed to be able to understand. If you spoke correctly they didn't really understand."

Interview with Ernie Richardson, May 27, 1984

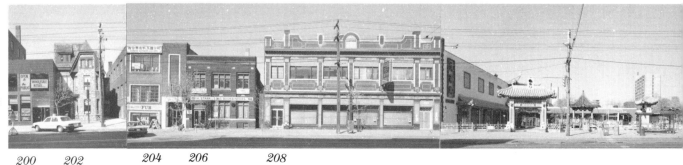

200   202   204   206   208

Early Morning Street Scene, Queen and Spadina, 1985
Lorne Fromer

Children on Cameron Street, 1969-70
Cameron and Queen, across the street from Alexandra Park.
Yuri Humphrey

**Bill and Marge,
Superintendents,
165 Spadina, 1974**
Raphael Bendahan

86

195   185   173

Canadian Imperial Bank of Commerce 165
Spadina

The small frame building at the northeast corner of Queen and Spadina was a hotel in the late 1880's, known variously as Brown's Hotel, Brewer's Hotel and the Avenue.

The present building was erected for the Bank of Hamilton, designed by architect G.W. Gouinlock in 1902. The storefronts that extend up the north side have been occupied by a variety of dress and fur merchants over the years. The restaurant on the corner of Bulwer Street, Abella's, was a well-known lunch counter and semi-official office for J.B. Salsberg, the local MPP. The second storey is presently occupied by small law firms.

The northwest corner of Spadina and Queen was a local gathering spot and, until the 1880's, marked the start of Spadina Avenue. The Salvation Army held street-corner concerts and

meetings here as far back as 1892. In the 1920's and 30's the corner became a battlefield between Communists and the Toronto Red Squad. In 1929, during a peaceful street-corner gathering for the Board of Control election, two speakers, George Andrews and Joe Farbey, were arrested and charged under the vagrancy section of the Criminal Code for "a disturbance in or near any street, road, highway or public place by screaming, swearing or singing, or by being drunk, or by impeding or incommodating peaceable passengers." They were sentenced to thirty days in the Don Jail. (Source: *The Little Band*, Lita-Rose Betcherman, Deneau, Ottawa, 1982)

Spadina, pre-1909
Looking north from Queen. The tree-lined boulevards were removed in the 1920's. The news kiosk on the left is presently run by the CNIB.
From *Greater Toronto Illustrated*, 1909, Public Archives Canada (C283)

**Excavation for King's
Court, June, 1984**
The south side of 192
Spadina, the Murray Build-
ing, is in the background.
Peter MacCallum

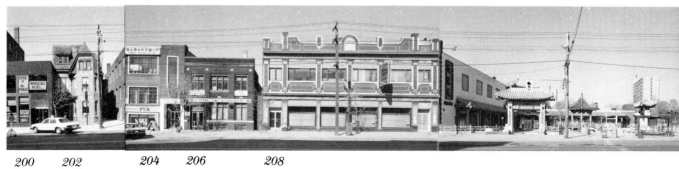

88

200   202   204   206   208

China Court *208-210 Spadina*

The site on the west side of Spadina Avenue was, in the late 1800's, the estate of Dr. Cook. Built as a grand mansion, it included a large formal garden with a fountain, a brick lodge at the entrance to the driveway, and stables enclosed by an iron fence.

Redeveloped in the 1920's, it became the General Motors sales and service centre for the Truck and Coach Division. In the late 1970's the GM operation was closed and sold. After a massive redesign, the site became the China Court shopping centre, featuring an Oriental motif and an exterior Chinese garden of bridges, ponds and ceremonial arches. The current owners propose to demolish the present structure and erect a major commercial-residential building.

Shoppers on Spadina, April, 1985
Looking southwest to China Court on the right.
Elizabeth Feryn

King's Court Under Construction, 188 Spadina, 1985
King's Court is one of a number of major developments on Spadina catering to the growing Chinese business and residential community.
Peter MacCallum

Department of Soldiers Civil Re-establishment, Keen's Building, 185 Spadina, c. 1918
Built in the 1910's at Spadina and Bulwer, Keen's Building was known locally as the Spadina Avenue Armouries. In the 1940's the Second Division RCCS and the ''A'' Corps RCCS were stationed on Spadina. The building is presently occupied by offices and the Toronto Trade Centre.
Peake & Whittingham, Public Archives Canada (PA 68101)

House Ghost, May, 1984
North side of Keen's Building, 185 Spadina.
Peter MacCallum

187-191 Spadina, June, 1940
The houses were demolished in 1940, but their ghosted form remains on the north wall of 185 Spadina.
City of Toronto Archives (Housing 714)

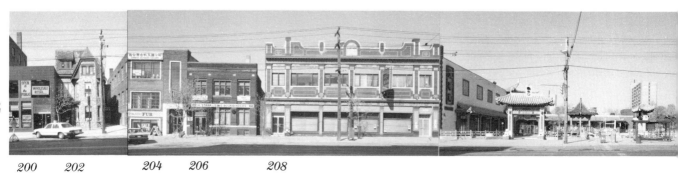

200   202   204   206   208

Labour Day Parade, September, 1957
Asbestos workers line up for the start of the parade.
Toronto Telegram, York University Archives (Box 354, 2347)

Milk Drivers and Dairy Employees Union, September, 1953
Labour Day Parade, Bulwer and Spadina.
Toronto Telegram, Ontario Archives (9977)

Majorettes, Labour Day Parade, September, 1977
Lorne Fromer

Jaakko (Carl) Lindala, 1912
A local businessman and leader of the Finnish Social Democratic Party, which congregated around Adelaide, Richmond and Spadina in the early 1900's. In 1907 Lindala ran for mayor on a Labour ticket, along with Jimmie Simpson for board of control. Simpson was elected and Lindala received approximately 12,000 votes.
Multicultural History Society, Ontario Archives (Finns 487)

Women's Gymnastics, Workers Sports Association, Alleyway, Alhambra Hall, 450 Spadina, 1925-26
From the left: Fanny Suckert Kalinsky, ?,?, Sonya Hershman (nee Layefsky) on bars, Albert Goldfile, ?, Lil Carson, Gertie (Mintz) Radin, Vera Radin.
Multicultural History Society, Ontario Archives (MSR 9161 #236)

Vapaus Bookstore *184 Spadina*

The head office of the Workers Sports Association was located at 184 Spadina. Formed in 1928, the WSA members were drawn from the Ukrainian, Jewish and Finnish youth groups and associated with the Young Communist League. The WSA saw its role as a "red" sports alternative to the YMCA-YWCA and by 1933 had 5,000 members across Canada. The association tried to encourage a wide variety of sports, but the major activity of the Toronto clubs was gymnastics. The Jewish Workers Sports Club held gymnastic competitions at the Alhambra Hall at 450 Spadina and used the rear lane for practice.

Weightlifting and wrestling activities were also popular at the WSA, where there was also accommodation for out-of-town athletes.

Members, dressed in white with a red belt and a red, star-shaped crest reading "Workers Sports Association," paraded for public events such as the Tim Buck Rally at Maple Leaf Gardens in 1934 and May Day Parades.

The Vapaus Bookstore run by Mr. Teckkala was on the ground floor of 184 Spadina and sold a wide range of Finnish books and newspapers. The Workers Restaurant upstairs was a co-operative Finnish restaurant and social centre.

Residence of Dr. William Ogden, 184 Spadina, c. 1910
One of the early stately homes of Spadina, this was later the Vapaus Bookstore and Workers Restaurant.
Baldwin Room, Metro Reference Library (T 11428)

Child Pioneers, 184 Spadina, 1935
The Vapaus Bookstore and Workers Restaurant were the centre of Finnish politics and social life on Spadina. The building has since been demolished.
Public Archives Canada (PA 126779)

Empire Clothing Building *197 Spadina*

The building on the northeast corner of Phoebe and Spadina was designed by Benjamin Brown for the Empire Clothing Company in 1923.

Originally, a row of elegant Victorian semi-detached houses stood on the site. An upper-class residential neighbourhood in the 1800's and 90's, this part of Spadina was a popular address for doctors and ministers.

**"The House of Stouts,"
Sapera Brothers Ltd., 197
Spadina**
Illustration by Robert
McRae, *Styles*, August,
1931.
Rare Book Room, Metro
Reference Library

**Mike Evangeli, Presser,
Shiffer-Hillman Co.,
197-205 Spadina,
September, 1978**
Shiffer-Hillman is one of the
longest-operating men's
clothing factories on
Spadina.
Jack Dobson, Globe & Mail

241   *235*   *229*   *227*   *225-223*   *221*

Residence of Dr. W.T. Stuart, 197 Spadina, 1891 The house was demolished in the 1920's, and the Empire Clothing Building was built on the site in 1926. It is now the location of Shiffer-Hillman.
Topley Collection, Public Archives Canada (PA 27239)

215

197-205

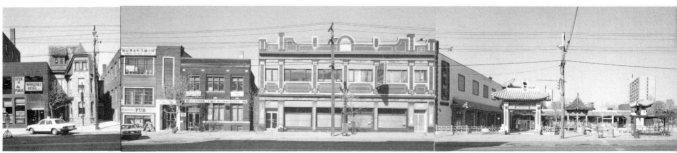

200   202   204   206   208

SPADINA AVENUE.
Between Grange Avenue and St Patrick Sts
1864.

Spadina Between Grange and St. Patrick (Dundas), 1864
The centre lane is marked Carr Lane, later known as Broadway Place (Willison Square).
Illustration by W.J. Thomson in *Robertson's Landmarks of Toronto*, Volume 3, 1896, Baldwin Room, Metro Reference Library

Canadian Seamen's Union Demonstration, 256 Spadina, late 1940's
The radical Canadian Seamen's Union (CSU) organized merchant seamen on the Great Lakes in the late 1930's and during the Second World War signed up the Canadian International Merchant Marine fleet. In 1948 the CSU was caught in a bitter strike against the Great Lake ship owners. The owners brought in the U.S.-based Seamen's International Union (SIU) led by Hal Banks. With the complicity of the Canadian government and the assistance of the owners, the SIU smashed the CSU and de-certified the union in 1949.
Helen Wasser, Canadian Tribune, Public Archives Canada (PA 93877)

orkmen Laying Sidewalk urbs, September, 1902
0 Spadina at Broadway ace (later Willison uare).
ty engineer photograph, y of Toronto Archives (Vol. 3, 6)

246   248   250   252   254   256

A Space, 204 Spadina, 1984
Founded in 1971 on St. Nicholas Street, A Space was the first artist-run parallel space in Canada. The gallery moved to Spadina in 1983 and was the location of the exhibition ''Spadina Ave.: A Photohistory'' in August-September, 1984. The exterior billboard installation by Cathy Daley is part of a series entitled ''Public Address.''
Peter MacCallum

Cultural Cutbacks Demonstration, March 16, 1985
A demonstration organized by the Toronto Artists Union.
Lorne Fromer

Injured Being Removed by Ambulance Attendants, February, 1931
The photograph was part of a montage illustrating a newspaper story entitled "Communists on Spadina Avenue Riot," February 26, 1931.
Toronto Telegram, Canada Wide

Free Speech

"Spadina Avenue is famous for what has been done there in the fight for freedom of speech. It is famous for the type of working people that walk there, to and fro, from the shop and factory, It is a social theatre. It is, more than all else, a battlefield. It has been such in years gone by, and it is today.

I remember how the Young Communist League adopted this broad avenue as the stage on which to put on many a good street meeting. Their youthful zeal smiled at the opposition of the foe.

It is a fine evening in April. A meeting is to be held at Dundas corner. The speaker mounts the box and exclaims: 'Comrades and fellow-workers.' Suddenly a loud 'Move on! Move on! You are too near the corner!' interrupts the eloquence of the speech. It is the police. The whole meeting moves a few paces from the corner and resumes its stance. The speaker resumes. He talks about unemployment and wage cuts. 'Move on!' order the police again. 'You are blocking traffic!' So once more the meeting shifts its 'soap box' and once more the speaker opens fire.

But the police are not finished. They come for the third time with their insistent 'move on.' But this time the officer says: 'You can't hold a meeting here.' He orders the meeting to disperse at once. And then commences a struggle on the street that was to be repeated many dozens of times. No one disperses. The speaker stays on the box. He is dragged down and conducted to the Black Maria. Another mounts the box to speak and is dragged away. But the crowd is in-creasing. The waves of excitement begin to roll up and down Spadina. The audience of a hundred or so around the orator as if by magic swells until there is a crowd of over a thousand people jamming the whole street. Traffic is now stopped. Other soap boxes come into use. The crowd shouts approval. They burst the sky with cheers. They surge around and around the box. They mill about. They will not leave the place. Five speakers have been taken away. And the sixth man is picked up by the police. This one is a stranger. No one knows his name, nor where he came from. He is thrown into the wagon.

In a short time I contacted the police station. The bail was set at $50 each for six men. 'Would I come and get them out?' The required $300 was soon collected.

We went to the station and there was fun. The stranger was in a rage at having been arrested in this fashion. On the street when told to 'move on' he had informed the police 'I'm an Irishman and, bejapers, I don't move for anyone.' With this the police had thrown him into the Black Maria. He was raging in the cell. 'What is this place I've got into? If I iver git out of here, I'll jine the Communists,' he shouted. All six were given thirty days in the Langstaff jail. There they had the job of landscaping the lawns and pathways in front of the prison. It turned out to be a work of art."

All My Life, Rev. A.E. Smith, Progress Books, Toronto, second edition, 1977.

Re-laying Bed for Street-car Tracks, May, 1919
Public works photograph, City of Toronto Archives (RDY 804)

City Workers, May, 1919
Looking south on Spadina. The Consolidated Glass Building is on the left.
Public works photograph, City of Toronto Archives (RDY 805)

246   248   250   252   254   256   260

Winter on Spadina,
c. 1912
Looking north from Dundas.
The Consolidated Glass
Building is on the right.
William James, City of Toronto
Archives (7066)

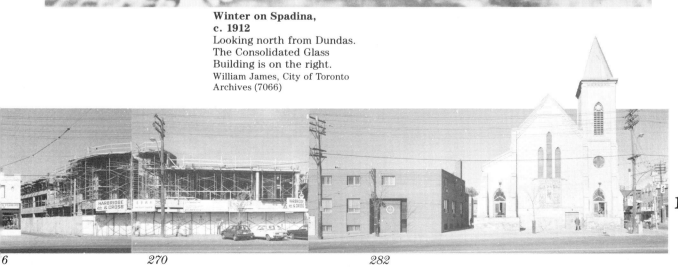

House *233-235 Spadina*

The house was built in the 1880's for a Mr. Huson Murray. It was briefly a funeral home in the 1910's. Since 1921 it has been rented for apartments and offices.

The house was purchased by the Starr family in 1950. The superintendent, Mike, was a well-recognized local figure who sat on the porch daily surveying the street. The house was often the scene of artists' gatherings. Graham Coughtry, the painter, and Irving Grossman, the architect, lived there.

The only extant house of the 1800's period left on Spadina Avenue, it is a small reminder of the street's former residential grandeur. Today, although sadly in need of repair, it retains the unusual feature of a small inner courtyard with a magnificent mountain ash tree.

Vacant House, 233-235 Spadina, June, 1984
The house, although vacant and in disrepair, remains one of the only examples of Spadina residential architecture of the late nineteenth century.
Peter MacCallum

283   281   277   273   271   269   267   265   263   261

Consolidated Glass Building, c. 1910
The house on the right is 235 Spadina.
Peake & Whittingham, Public Archives Canada (PA 68069)

Cast Iron Doorway, Consolidated Glass Building, 239-241 Spadina, May, 1984
Peter MacCallum

The Consolidated Plate Glass Building
241 Spadina

The Consolidated Plate Glass Company was formed by the merger of several companies in 1893, under the directorship of John W. Hobbs. It imported and sold plate, sheet and ornamental glass, as well as painters' and glaziers' supplies.

In 1910 William Steele, an industrial architect based in Pittsburgh, designed a five-storey brick warehouse for Consolidated Plate Glass on Spadina Avenue, at a cost of $60,000. His other major industrial buildings in the city were the Toronto Carpet Factory on King Street West, and the Eaton's warehouse on Bay Street (demolished).

The Beaux-Arts building facade is of terra cotta, red sandstone and brick. The entrance arch was designed with a cast-iron gate, which enclosed a small portico with four steps. The interior post-beam construction with wood floor, stairwell wainscotting and ceiling, remains intact.

The building is presently owned by HonCon Development Company, with Icebox Flowers and the Chinese Canadian Intercultural Association as the main tenants of the upper floors. The original facade has been altered by the introduction of a centre stair to the Formal Creations shop on the main floor.

St. Elizabeth of Hungary Church *282 Spadina*
The site at the southwest corner of Spadina and
St. Patrick (Dundas) was originally part of the
Denison family estate, which included most of
the area west of Spadina where Kensington Market now stands. Arthur Denison designed the
low Anglican church and school on the site, "a
plain, quadrangular, red brick edifice with very
scant pretensions to architectural beauty"
(*Toronto: Past and Present Until 1882*,
J. Mulvany, 1884). The church was officially
opened in January, 1884, having cost $17,000.

The building was purchased by the Roman
Catholic Archdiocese in 1943 and was rededicated to St. Elizabeth of Hungary. The parish
became the centre for the local Hungarian Catholic community, which had previously had a
small church on Grange Street.

In 1956, with the suppression of the Hungarian uprisings, St. Elizabeth's became the
organizational centre for the refugee airlift, as
the headquarters of the Canadian Hungarian
Federation in Toronto. St. Elizabeth's and Spadina Avenue were often the first contact in
Canada for newly arrived refugees. The church
and parish hall became the religious and social
centre for the refugees.

To accommodate the enlarged parish, the
church proper was renovated in 1958-59 and
1963, and a new rectory at 280 Spadina was
built in 1967.

Due to the declining numbers in the Hungarian community within the downtown core,
the Roman Catholic Archdiocese of Toronto
recently sold the site to the Hing Lung Corporation. It is awaiting demolition to make room for
an eight- to ten-storey commercial/residential
complex. The proposed completion date for the
project is 1986-87.

Why don't you

HELP HUNGARY!

C.F.R.B. Comment by J. COLLINGWOOD READE

"Send not to find for whom the bell tolls. It tolleth for thee." The funeral bell which rings today for the Hungarian dead in Budapest is not a remote sound telling the doom of distant foreigners speaking a strange tongue. The bell is tolling for our brethren in the Commonwealth of Man who loving freedom more than life, advanced against the bestial troops of the proletarian dictatorship with their arms outstretched to show that they were defenseless, and without weapons. Some it is true, were armed and there must have been an effective underground organization engaged in gunrunning. But many chose certain death rather than the natural course of life under conditions imposed by a government amenable to the dictates of the Soviet Union. This amazing exhibition of the immortality of the free human spirit — of its strength, its courage and its determination to survive as a free spirit or perish, is or should be both an inspiration and a warning to us all."

Flame of Freedom by JUDITH ROBINSON, The Telegram, Oct. 26,1956

"The struggle begun, the hope of freedom flames high in the darkness for those who have begun it and they fight on. The stories of it come as from a far distance in time as well as space.

Yet it is being made now, it concerns us all.

Freedom, for Hungarians, and Poles is not something to be enjoyed. It is something to be remembered and regained. It is a possession infinitely precious and precarious, won and lost and won again by succeeding generations. It is an idea more real than the realities of comfort and security and of greater worth than life."

Support the fight for freedom through the

CANADIAN ⚜ HUNGARIAN
FEDERATION

c/o St. Elizabeth Church of Hungary, 519 Dundas St. W. Toronto, EM. 8-4149

246   248   250   252   254   256   260

Help Hungary
Joseph Racz distributing
leaflets (opposite page) pro-
testing Russian intervention
in the Hungarian revolt in
front of St. Elizabeth's of
Hungary Church, November
13, 1956.
Toronto Telegram, York University Archive (Box 210, 1559)

**Hungarian Refugees on
the Spadina Bus, Decem-
ber, 1956**
The refugees are on their
way to St. Elizabeth's, the
headquarters of the Cana-
dian-Hungarian Federation.
Toronto Telegram, York University Archives (Box 210, 1559)

**First Communicants with
Father Paul Tiszai, St.
Elizabeth's, 1952**
Multicultural History Society,
Ontario Archives (6465, #73)

Red Spadina, c. 1930
Demonstration outside the
Standard Theatre at Spa-
dina and Dundas, probably
part of the "Free Speech"
campaign. Mounted
policemen (on the
left were a
common sight
on Spadina during
the 1930's.
Toronto Telegram,
York Univer-
sity Archives

Street Corner Speakers *Dundas and Spadina*

"Many socialists were street-corner speakers, preaching socialism on street corners, and I especially enjoyed speaking on one street corner on Dundas and Spadina. All the Jews were so much upset because of an old man singer, a *mishimit* — he was a Christian missionary. Even non-religious socialists were negative; we disliked a Jew being a *Yeshiva butcher* in the young days, coming here, joining the missionaries, then using it as a job to try to convert the Jews in the Jewish neighbourhood to Christianity. So I always enjoyed taking the next corner with about a couple of dozen of our socialists and speaking on a box while he had three, four people listening. I enjoyed standing there on a box and talking, preaching, telling them to be good trade unionists, fighting for shorter hours and better wages, against exploitation of the sweat shops, and also calling them to join the ranks of the socialist movement because we'll never have any freedom or economical security unless we bring socialism. And I used to say, 'Why, this fellow over there is promising you pie-in-the-sky. We promise you something now!' We had a wonderful time with that missionary, but the poor fellow was so disgusted because we were capturing every passerby. So the street corners were our means for years. We had dozens of our fellow activists in the *Arbeiterring*, in the trade union movement, in the socialist movement."

Sam Beckman

Born in 1886 in the Ukraine, he participated in the revolutionary events in Russia in 1905 and was deeply affected by the anti-Jewish pogroms. He came to Canada in 1908 and was active in the Socialist Party and union organizing.

The Great War and Canadian Society, an Oral History, Daphne Read, ed., New Hogtown Press, Toronto, 1978.

292   294   296   298 298a 300   300a   302

**Fur Workers General
Strike, June 16, 1958**
Seven hundred fur workers
march on Spadina south of
Dundas, on strike against
eighty-five employers.
Toronto Telegram, York University Archives (Box 477, 3159)

322   324   326   328   332   334   336   338   340   346

Standard Theatre *287 Spadina*

The first building on the northeast corner of
Dundas and Spadina was a small frame church,
the Methodist New Connection Church, built in
1871. In 1876 the congregation bought land at
College and Spadina and moved the frame structure up the Avenue on rollers. The property was
then bought by Dr. H.H. Moorehead, who built a
grand house, which he lived in for over thirty-
five years.

The house was demolished in the late 1910's
and a theatre was designed by Benjamin Brown.
The Standard Theatre opened on August 18,
1921, and was one of the finest Yiddish theatres
in North America. It was financed by selling
shares to the local Yiddish-speaking community
and was managed by Isodore Axler. The theatre
had its own stock company, which did everything from the Yiddish masters to melodramas of
low comedy and high tragedy. A touring company from New York would present the classics
in Yiddish — Shakespeare, Gorky, Strindberg,
Adler.

The theatre was also the scene of many lectures and meetings. In 1929 the Toronto police
broke up a meeting to commemorate the death
of Lenin and arrested Max Schur and another
speaker for addressing the audience in a language other than English. Tear gas was thrown
and Becky Buhay, who had taken the chair, was
overcome on the stage.

On December 4, 1933, members of the Progressive Arts Club mounted the agit-prop play,
Eight Men Speak. The play, written by Oscar
Ryan, Ed Cecil-Smith, Frank Love and Mildred
Goldberg, had a cast of twenty-five. It used a
melange of styles — naturalistic, episodic, agit-
prop recitation — and attacked the imprison-
ment of the Communist Party leaders. The first
performance sold out, and a second performance
was scheduled. The Toronto Police Commission
threatened to revoke the theatre's film licence if
the hall was rented to the Progressive Arts Club
again. The play became part of the campaign
which led to the release of the eight men in
1934.

In 1935 the theatre changed its name to
the Strand and re-opened as a movie-house, although it continued to have theatrical performances and lectures on Sundays. In celebration
of the end of the War, it was renamed the Victory and became a burlesque house. Notorious in
its day, the Victory was a hang-out for university students and artists who often used it as a
subject for paintings and photography.

Victory Burlesque, 1971
Peter MacCallum

**Robert Markle and Miss
Angel Eyes, Victory Bur-
lesque Dressing Room,
1962**
Michel Lambeth, Public
Archives Canada

In 1975 the theatre was sold to Hang Hing
Investments. The building was redesigned by
Mandel Spachman, who altered the entrance
and added a basement dining room. It re-opened
as the Golden Harvest Theatre, just as the Dundas and Spadina corner was becoming a centre
for the Asian community in Toronto.

110

Shopsowitz Delicatessen and Catering, 295 Spadina, 1950's
Exterior night view after the deli was enlarged to include two storefronts. The building was demolished in 1983 and replaced in 1985. Shopsy's Ltd.

Corned Beef Madeleine

"On Spadina again, caught in the downpour, against which I did not lower my head, crossing block after block along a route taken a hundred years ago by colonial soldiers marching to Fort York. I was not interested in this street as history. Nor were the Chinese and Portuguese and West Indians, I thought, who all about me were hurrying to take shelter. Their expressions were the same as ours when we arrived on this street: a look that was empty of the past and that suffered the present. But their eyes gleamed as if reflecting the future that was visible all about them — a future of sturdy clothes and well-stocked stores and motor cars. Even in the rain I could see that what appeared to be new shops and buildings were only facades over the old: larger windows, bright tile, some stone work. I felt my past had not been erased, just covered over and given new names in other languages.

Just before Dundas Street my attention was caught by a large sign across the street, *Shopsy's*. Despite pangs of hunger, I could not bring myself to go inside. I kept walking, swallowing streams of saliva. In my time it had been a small delicatessen. I remembered Shopsy's parents. They stood at the steam table from morning to night, pale and patient, wearing long white aprons, their faces moist from the steamer. They were unfailingly benign towards children. The rear of the little narrow store opened onto a corridor that led to the lobby of the Yiddish theatre and patrons could buy sandwiches, pop and candy at intermission. Once, out of curiosity, I went through Shopsy's into a dark lobby, found the theatre doors open and watched a rehearsal. No one but me, apparently, knew that the doors were kept open during rehearsals. I got to know the actors and actresses and had the honor of being sent for corned-beef sandwiches, one of which was for me as a tip. That sandwich! Elevated to Proustian heights by a Toronto poet as the 'corned-beef madeleine.' From that time on, all I have to do is bite into a sandwich and I am once more in the empty dark theatre, the actors come on stage and I live out again the old melodramas of incestuous love, *dybbuks*, white slavery, lovers parted by a cruel fate. ..."

Basic Black with Pearls, Helen Weinzweig, Anansi, Toronto, 1980.

The Chinese Community

The Chinese originally came to Canada as cheap labour; by 1881 there were 50,000, the majority working on the railroad for one dollar a day. After the railway was completed in the late 1880's, the Canadian government, prodded by B.C. anti-Chinese sentiment and trade union lobbies, restricted further immigration by imposing a head tax.

The early Chinese community was centred in Vancouver and Victoria, where anti-Oriental racism was common. After 1907, when Vancouver's Chinatown was ransacked by rioters, the Chinese started to move east.

By 1910 there were over 1,000 Chinese living in Toronto around Queen and King streets. The small Chinatown was constantly harassed and restricted because of Anglo-Canadian beliefs that all Chinese were opium dealers, gamblers and white-slavers; in reality, many of the Chinese operated small, family-run hand laundries, open seven days a week from 6 a.m. to 9 p.m.

In 1923 the Chinese Immigration Act virtually terminated Chinese immigration for twenty-four years. After the Second World War, when China was a Canadian ally and Chinese-Canadians were conscripted into the army, the Chinese Immigration Act was repealed.

The Toronto Chinese community increased slowly in the 1950's and 60's. Demolition of the Queen Street West area for the new City Hall and Sheraton Centre pushed the community north onto Dundas and then west. The residential Chinese community joined the fight to stop the Spadina Expressway. In the 1970's a Save Chinatown committee was formed in the Dundas/Elizabeth area to oppose high-rise development and plans to widen Dundas.

The changes in the Immigration Act in the 1970's brought new Asian immigrants to Toronto, many from Hong Kong. Later the Vietnamese boat people, many of whom were of Chinese origin, arrived. With the recent tightening of family immigration policy and a new stress on entrepreneurial skills and investment capital, there has been an influx of Hong Kong-based investment ($2.5 billion between 1980 and 1983) centring in real estate. Recent Chinese immigrants are rebuilding moribund shops, restaurants and theatres and revitalizing social and economic patterns. The public street life has changed dramatically; shopping and eating out are important elements in the social life of the community. The new Chinatown has become one of the most active street scenes in Toronto.

Mrs. Woo, Happy Meat Market, 352 Spadina, 1985
Pamela Gawn

292   294   296 298 298a 300   300a   302

Street Portraits, 1984
Isaac Applebaum

Adoration of the Prince, 287-289 Spadina, April, 1985
The former underground dance club and disco in the basement of the Golden Harvest Theatre, now the Van Canh Restaurant.
Pamela Gawn

Unloading Product for Tai Ping Mart, Spadina and Dundas, April, 1985
From the left: Kem Seek Hoi, Chow and Tang Chhoa, store clerks.
Pamela Gawn

114

**Press Room, "Sing Tao"
Newspaper, 357 Spadina,
June, 1984**
"Sing Tao" is the major
Chinese-language news-
paper in Toronto.
Peter MacCallum

115

Sammy Taft, 1981
Sammy Taft originally
opened at 340 Spadina. He
retired in 1985, and the
store has since been sold.
June Clark Greenberg

Sammy Taft, the World Famous Hatter
303 Spadina

"If I'm famous it's because I've been here so
long, and I talk to people. I sit outside and I say
hello to everyone. If someone walks by I
acknowledge them. I built my business mouth-
to-mouth — one person tells the other. I don't
have to advertise, I don't need advertising. I get
more out of advertising my way, than people
spending money for ads.

Sure it's been a nice thrill for me to bring the
whole world to Spadina Avenue, the names that
come out of their way, just to come and say
hello, to send their regards. I've been on CBC so
many times. I'm on television, radio programs.
It's just routine. Doesn't faze me one way or the
other ... I just do what I'm supposed to do."

Interview with Sammy Taft, May 23, 1984

Ben Barshtz and his Children, Fay, Sam and Joe, Standard Barber Shop, 305 Spadina, c. 1920
The Barshtz family orchestra played at local weddings and bar mitzvahs and were known for their Klezmer music (traditional eastern European Jewish folk music).
Stella Rudolph (nee Barsh)

Slacks Wholesale Dry Goods, 323 Spadina, August, 1981
From the left: Marty, Bertha and Isaac Slack.
June Clark Greenberg

Canadian Winter, 1960-61

Up Spadina, feet like the slow end
of a mutt sniffing from trashcan to pole,
(smutty, scruffy, sour-fat on a thin dole,
pausing whole minutes to lick his behind)
regularly — rain, tea-weak sun, or blinding
snow-glutted poundage of a cold gale —
grey, jawdroopy with ragged lips, the pale
men past forty peg to the breadline.

They've washed in the dirty water of boredom
and in thinly conscious ways are still here;
but predictable in fluctuation
as spasms of malarial fever
or winged ant exodi. My bizarre sir
stop a minute! think of the word "human."

I've Tasted My Blood, Poems 1956-1968, Milton
Acorn, Ryerson Press, Toronto, 1969.

**Waiting, 294 Spadina,
1975**
Raphael Bendahan

292   294   296 298 298a 300 300a   302

Pedestrian, 494A Dundas, April, 1985
The entrance to the Wai Wai Trading Co., Dundas and Spadina.
Pamela Gawn

Pedestrian Outside Liquor Store at 291 Spadina, 1978
David Levine

The Toronto Jewish Folk Choir

In 1925 a group of Jewish factory workers founded the Freiheit Gezangs Farein (Freedom Choral Society), under the leadership of Hyman Riegelhaupt. Their first annual concert was held in 1926 at the Alhambra Hall on Spadina. Renamed the Toronto Jewish Folk Choir in 1934, the group has maintained its spring concert tradition.

The Jewish-American composer Jacob Schaeffer came to conduct the group in 1928 and led the choir in Massey Hall in 1935 and again in 1936 for the performance of his *Tzvei Brider* (Two Brothers) set to I.L. Peretz's poem. It is said that when Schaeffer rehearsed this work with the choir on Sunday mornings at the Labor League, people lined up outside to listen.

In 1939 the Vienna-born musician Emil Gartner took over leadership of the choir. Under Gartner the choir grew to well over one hundred members. He directed works by Handel, Mendelssohn, Dvorak, Prokofiev and Shostakovitch among others and invited such singers as Igor Gorin, Regina Resnick, Paul Robeson, Jan Peerce and Jenny Tourel to appear as guest soloists. John Weinzweig, Louis Applebaum and other Canadian composers were commissioned to write works for the choir, and outstanding artists like Lois Marshall performed with it. Throughout the years, Fagel Gartner was the accompanist.

After Emil Gartner's death, the choir lived through difficult years but has maintained its efforts to bring progressive Jewish and general culture to its audiences.

292   294   296   298 298a 300   300a   302

ליבעטע קאָנווענשאָן פֿו   מעמבלאָכמער פאָבאָא.
                                                                              452 קויז וועסט

Poalei Zion Group, 1913
Ber Borochov, centre.
Toronto Jewish Congress
Archives (2913)

322   324   326   328   332   334   336   338   340   346

Phil Ladovsky
Apartment, 340 Spadina,
1983.
Lorne Fromer

Ron Switzer, Scriptwriter
Apartment, 352 Spadina,
1978.
Lorne Fromer

United Bakers, *338 Spadina*
As early as the 1830's, the site north of Glen
Baillie Place was occupied by private homes,
such as that of Sir Francis Hincks, the railroad
entrepreneur and reformer. The present three-
storey building was erected in the late 1880's.

In 1920 Aaron and Sarah Ludovsky bought
the store and apartment and opened the United
Bakeries Restaurant, which had been located on
Terauley (Bay Street) since 1912. The name
United Bakers Dairy was drawn from an early
attempt by Ludovsky and others to organize
bakery workers in Toronto. In the 1940's their
son, Herman Ludovsky, took over management
of the restaurant, which he continues to run
with his son Philip and his daughter Ruth.

122

292   *294*   *296*   *298*   *298a*   *300*   *300a*   *302*

**Walerstein's Ice Cream
Parlor, 332 Spadina,
c. 1921**
Esther Walerstein standing
outside her father's shop.
The entrance to Glen Baillie
Place is on the left. The
store is now occupied by
United National Hardware.
Toronto Jewish Congress
Archives (2533)

123

322   324   326   328   332   334   336   338   340   346

Emma Goldman in Her Study, 1930's
S. Flechine, Paris (photographer), family memento of Merle Langbord Levin

Emma Goldman

Emma Goldman (1869-1940), the well-known feminist, anarchist and critic, lived in Toronto for a number of years in the 1920's and 30's. Goldman had lost her U.S. citizenship, and Toronto was close to her family in upper New York state. She had many friends and supporters in the anarchist branch of the Workmen's Circle and in the local Italian anarchist community.

She lived for a time in a semi-detached house on Spadina south of Harbord, and later at 665-669 Spadina, now the Wing On Funeral Home.

Her lectures at the Hygeia Hall on Elm Street promoted planned parenthood and legalization of birth control. The local medical health officer commented favourably. The press covered her lectures, revelling in her attacks on Stalin and the Soviet Union. She lectured at the Standard and the Labor Lyceum on drama, anarchism and youth:

> In all the sciences today, in art, literature and music you find the same desire to get away from the bonds of academic and confining formulas. The futurists, the cubists, what have they been but anarchists, rebels against the coercion of burdening tradition? In music — why music is filled with ultra-revolutionary movements. Jazz? Yes, jazz is anarchistic, the very spirit of youth, essentially a revolt against outworn traditions and restrictions. (Toronto *Star*, April 28, 1927)

A Very Interesting Lecture
by
Emma
GOLDMAN
on the theme
"THE YOUTH IN REVOLT"
will take place
Sunday, 4th of April (1937)
8:30 p.m.
Labor Lyceum
346 Spadina Ave.
Don't lose the opportunity to hear Emma Goldman
on this theme before her departure from Canada
Arranged by Branch 339, Arbeiter Ring (Workmen's Circle).
Toronto Jewish Congress Archives (76-12/1)

Goldman died of a paralytic stroke at the home of friends at 295 Vaughan Road on May 14, 1940. On May 15, her body was taken to the Labor Lyceum. The three-hour memorial ceremony overflowed onto Spadina. Her body was shipped to Chicago, where she was buried with the Haymarket Martyrs of 1887.

**Streetcar Stop, Nassau
and Spadina, 1920's**
Toronto Transit Commission
(3523)

Glen Baillie Place, July, 1984
Located between Dundas and St. Andrew's, Glen Baillie Place is a small alley and inner court surrounded by small two-storey row houses.
Peter MacCallum

Residence of Sir Francis Hincks, approximately 332 Spadina at Glen Baillie, c. 1885
Sir Francis Hincks, railway entrepreneur and later minister of finance, lived here in the 1830's. The unusual Regency-style house was demolished in the 1880's and replaced by the present 3-storey storefronts.
Baldwin Room, Metro Reference Library (T 11310)

320-328 Spadina

Situated at Glen Baillie Place and Spadina, the three-storey building with an unusual balcony over the centre doorway was erected in the 1890's. The building is known locally as the building in which Emma Goldman died, though she actually died on Vaughan Road.

In the 1930's and 40's the building was called the Hertel Building. The second and third floors were offices and private social clubs such as the Tribel, the Aster, Club Rex and the Independent Mutual Benefit Society. Semi-professional theatres, the Belmont Theatre and the Plaquests Group had rehearsal space and held performances here. In the 1960's and 70's, artists and photographers had studios in the building. The main floor stores have housed a succession of delicatessens since the 1930's: the Welcome Restaurant, La Bell's, Litman's and, since 1948, Switzer's.

292   294   296 298 298a 300 300a   302

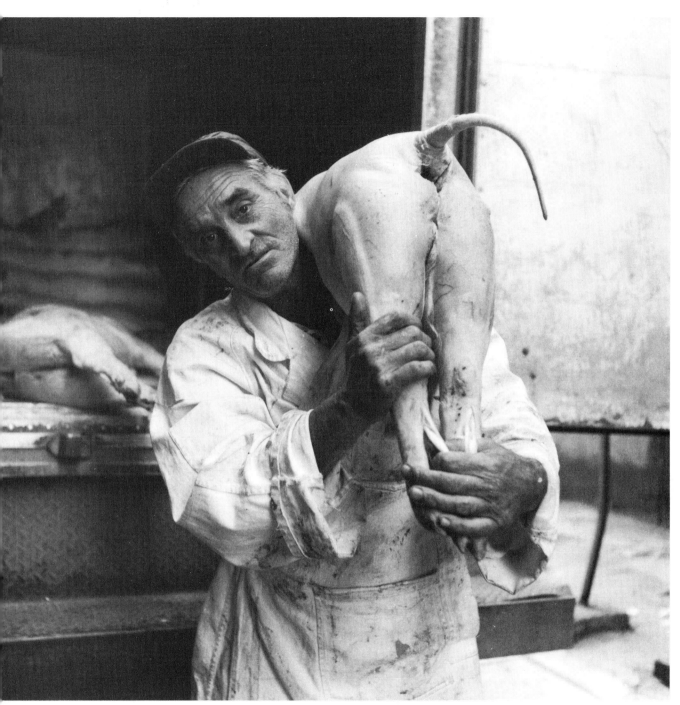

**Delivering Pigs, Glen
Baillie and Spadina, 1977**
Raphael Bendahan

Labor Lyceum

Incorporated in 1913 as a non-profit corporation, the Labor Lyceum sought to promote trade unionism and raise money for a trade union centre. With the assistance of Henry Dworkin, a local travel agent, the Lyceum sold five-dollar shares to trade unions and individuals to enable the group to purchase two houses on the southwest corner of Spadina and St. Andrew's. In 1929 a new front and meeting rooms were added. The Lyceum was the headquarters for the international needle trades unions (i.e. those not affiliated with the Communist Party): International Ladies Garment Workers (ILGWU), Cloakmakers and Dressmakers, Amalgamated Clothing Workers, Fur Workers, Hat, Cap and Millinery Workers Union and fraternal organizations such as the Workmen's Circle and the Socialist Farband, who used the facility for concerts, lectures, dances and performances.

As the major centre of trade union and cultural activities, the Labor Lyceum was an important gathering point. Emma Goldman spoke there in the 1930's. During the Second World War the United Labor Brass Band and the Finnish orchestra of Gunnar Gustafson would play for dances. In the late 1940's the Lyceum acquired a licence to serve beer.

In the early 1950's the exterior was refinished and a second-floor hall added. By 1972 the trade unions had moved to 23-25 Cecil Street, the site

International Fur Workers Union, Locals 40 and 100, 1934
Max Federman (seated fourth from left) continues as the manager of Locals 58 and 82 of the Fur Workers. The unusual facial appearance of the group is probably due to the overly strong studio lighting.
Famous Studio, Fur, Leather, Shoe & Allied Workers Union

Union Contract Signing Ceremony, c. 1940
Seated from the left: Max Charney, Nathan Cohen, Abe Kirzner, ?, Nat Laurie, President of Manufacturer's Association, J.L. Cohen, Ab Magerman, ?, ?. Rear: ?, ?, Jack Spivak, ?, ?.
International Ladies Garment Workers Union

of the original Jewish Old Folks Home, and sold the building.

After major renovations in an Oriental theme, the building was re-opened as a restaurant. In the past few years the building has been occupied by the Yen Pin, the Gengis Khan Mongolian Barbeque, Paul's Deep Sea Szechuan Palace and, most recently, the President. The building is again under renovation and will re-open as part of an international chain of Chinese restaurants.

Labour Day Banquet, ILGWU, Labor Lyceum, 1940
Ab Magerman at the microphone.
International Ladies Garment Workers Union

322   324   326   328   332   334   336   338   340   346

First Annual Fruit Ball,
'27
...ella Rudolph (nee Barsh)

...unnar Gustafson's Dance
...rchestra, c. 1930
...ated from the left: Max
...omaki, Lempi Halonen,
...unnar Gustafson, Suo-
...ela. Rear: Sigurd Ilomaki,
...mer Kingelin, Arvi King-
...in, Hannula, August Blom.
...lticultural History Society,
...tario Archives (MSR 7382 #1)

Furriers' Float, Labour
Day Parade, 1957
Fur, Leather, Shoe & Allied
Workers Union

322   324   326   328   332   334   336   338   340   346

St. Andrew's and Spadina

The three-storey building at the northeast corner of St. Andrew's and Spadina was erected for W.E. Dunn in 1890. It was designed by William G. Storm, one of the major romance revival architects of the period who also designed University College and St. Andrew's Church at King and Simcoe.

The five stores which form the complex were elaborately detailed in their brickwork and wrought-iron cornices. The focus of the building is the south corner, which extends onto St. Andrew's and is defined by a roof-line corner pinnacle inscribed "ERECTED 1890."

The three storefronts were known for over thirty years as Stitsky's Imports. A painted sign on the north end of the building remains. Rotman's has been located on the southeast corner since the 1930's and is one of the oldest permanent establishments on Spadina.

Labour Day Parade, 1957
Looking to St. Andrew's and Spadina.
Fur, Leather, Shoe & Allied Workers Union

Five Storefronts, 350-358 Spadina, 1890
The stores were designed by W.G. Storm, architect for W.E. Dunn.
Architectural drawing, Horwood Collection, Ontario Archives (Storm 733)

350   352   354   356   358   360   368   370   372   374

**Mr. Rotman, Rotman's
Men's Wear, 350 Spadina,
July, 1984**
The Rotman family has had
businesses on Spadina since
the 1920's.
Peter MacCallum

376   378   380   382   384   386   388   390   392   394   396   398

News Kiosk, September, 1938
Looking east to the Hebrew Men of England Synagogue, from St. Andrew's.
Public works photograph, City of Toronto Archives (RDY 1500)

No Karate, 339 Spadina, 1980
David Levine

377   375   373   371   369   367   365   363   361   359   357   355 355a 353

**Opening of the Hebrew
Men of England
Synagogue, 1921**
From the left: Jacob Gordon, ?, Cantor Bernard
Wladowsky.
Ottawa Jewish Historical
Society, Public Archives Canada
(C 57258)

347   345   343   341   339   337   333   331   329   327

327-329 Spadina

In 1875 the small Spadina Avenue Congregational Church was erected on this site. This original church was added onto the back of the new building begun in 1888. The new church, built of white brick, seated 775 and included a gallery on three sides and a choir platform. The ceiling, 37 feet in height, was constructed with a single span and triple-barred arches and divided by plaster ribs and purlins. In 1921, because of declining numbers, the congregation passed a resolution to unite with the Dale Presbyterian Church of Queen Street, and the church was

Women Weeping at the Site of the Fire, Hebrew Men of England Synagogue, July, 1960
Toronto Telegram, Canada Wide

Western Congregational Church, 1890's
Baldwin Room, Metro Reference Library (T 10840)

377   375   373   371   369   367   365   363   361   359   357   355 355a 353

sold for $70,000. The congregation split over the merger, and a rump church met for a brief time at the Christadelphian Church on Cecil Street. In 1926 they rented a church at College and Lippincott, with Salem Bland as minister. The congregation dissolved in the early 1930's.

The church building was purchased by the Beis Harness Anshei England, who were orthodox East European Jews, known in English as the Hebrew Men of England. The building was renovated by architect B. Swartz and adapted to a more Eastern European architectural style. The "Londoner Schul," as it was known locally, was inaugurated in August, 1922, with a seat sale to its members.

In July, 1960, a fire destroyed the building and all its records. The property was sold and the congregation re-established briefly in north Toronto. The site was redeveloped in 1963 as the New Paramount Hotel, with a two-storey, international-style building of four storefronts to the south.

Four Storefronts, 327-329 Spadina, June, 1984
Previously the site of the Hebrew Men of England Synagogue; now Silverstein & Sons Ltd.
Peter MacCallum

Hebrew Men of England Synagogue, c. 1947
D.M. Derry, Baldwin Room, Metro Reference Library
(T 10841)

347   345   343   341   339   337   333   331   329   327

Hyman's Book and Art Shop *371 Spadina*
Ben Zion Hyman (1914-1985), with his wife Fanny, operated Hyman's Book and Art Shop from 1925 until 1973.

The shop was open from 8:30 a.m. to 1:00 a.m. every day except Saturday and had a mimeograph machine, pop cooler, newspapers and a bar mitzvah registry. It sold Yiddish and Hebrew books, Judaica, tickets for the Standard Theatre, stationery and school supplies.

Mr. Hyman had been trained as an engineer in Russia and at the University of Toronto, but had never found work as an engineer.

Hyman's Book and Art Shop, 1925
Ben Zion Hyman outside his shop, which later moved to 412 Spadina.
Toronto Jewish Congress Archives (1171)

350   352   354   356   358   360   368   370   372   374

Morning, 388 Spadina, 1985
Looking south from Fortune Housewares, with Mr. Paul Menceles, the owner, on the right.
Elizabeth Feryn

Rutherford's Cut Rate Drug Store, 400 Spadina, c. 1917
Wilson & Larkin, Baldwin Room, Metro Reference Library (T 12350)

**Lowe's Wine and Liquors,
376 Spadina, 1890's**
From the left: Mr. McBride,
Charles Low, Maria Jane
Low. Local, privately owned
liquor stores were common
in Toronto before the 1916
Prohibition Act.
George Low

376   378   380   382   384   386   388   390   392   394   396   398

SPADINA AVENUE.
Between Baldwin and Nassau Sts.
❊ 1864 ❊

Spadina, Baldwin and Nassau, 1864
Illustration by W.J. Thomson for *Robertson's Landmarks of Toronto,* Volume 3, 1896.
Baldwin Room, Metro Reference Library

Lowe's Wine and Liquors, 378 Spadina, 1880's
The building still exists, although the semi-detached houses on the north side were later moved to Baldwin Street. The gas lamp stand on the corner was one of the last of its kind in Toronto.
George Low

Star Cleaners, 378 Spadina, May, 1954
The basic building has remained untouched since the 1880's, except for minor alterations in the street-front windows.
J.V. Salmon, Baldwin Room, Metro Reference Library (S1-397)

400   402   404   406   408   410   412   414   416   418   420   422   424   426   428   430

Branch 6, Labor League, c. 1930
There were four women's branches of the Labor League, numbers 6, 14, 23 and 8. Front row from the left: Rose Cohen, H. Cohen, Goldie Hoffman, Katie Horovitz, Manny Rose, Rae Watson. Second row: ?, Mrs. Goldberg, Mrs. Kavater, Mrs. Zalinsky, Fanny Horovitch, ?, Mrs. Neiman. Third row: Rosie Bain, Mrs. Coopersmith, Mrs. Loft, Mrs. Volkofski, ?, Mrs. Milton, Bella Marcuse, Mrs. Fine, Minnie Vinig, Sara Schwartz. Fourth row: ?, ?, Lilly Starkman, ?, ?, ?, ?. Fifth row: Mrs. Zabner, ?, Mrs. Benstock, Lily Gershovitz, Mrs. Ladofsky, ?, Mrs. Dachkofsky, Mrs. Shilman, Rose Gluck, Esther Bitell.
Toronto Jewish Congress Archives (261)

Women Activists

"Women were really active in the area. I remember Fanny, an early organizer for the ILGWU — 'the Union.' She was a finisher. She was single, her whole life just seemed to be organizing. Pearl Wedro, she came from Winnipeg to Toronto in about 1926-27. She was a furrier. Pearl was a socialist and executive member of the Fur Workers.

Then there was Mrs. Coopersmith, a character — a mother, a grandmother — she started organizing the Mother's Day celebrations in the Labor League. She was all bent over, she had something wrong with her spine, but as long as I knew her she was involved in everything, plus she looked after the store on Spadina and her family.

There was also a Housewives Movement in '32-34 — they organized around the Jewish meat stores in Kensington. Inflation was awful. Prices went up two or three cents on a quart of milk, while salaries were dropping. Before the war things were pretty grim."

Interview with Lily Ilomaki, April, 1985

May Day, 1954
Looking west to College and Spadina. May Day parades and events had been an important part of local life since the 1910's, although they were banned in the early 1930's.
Toronto Telegram, York University Archives

429   425   421   419 417   415   413   411   409   407   405   403   401   399   397   3

Union Representatives, May Day Parade, 1936
The 1936 May Day demonstration drew an estimated 40,000 people and included bands, trade unions, political groups, choirs and sports associations. Max Dolgoy is in the centre with Sam Rottenberg on the right.
Multicultural History Society, Ontario Archives (MRS 8418 #13)

Founders and Directors of the Workmen's Circle, 1943
Toronto Jewish Congress Archives (3054)

The Workmen's Circle

"The Workmen's Circle is the largest Yiddish fraternal organization in the world. It was comprised of various political factions until the convention of 1922 here in Toronto at the King Edward Hotel. We expelled the Communist Party because they tried to take over. In Toronto we lost 1,000 members. They weren't called the Communist Party then; they were called Marxists and Trotskyites. After we threw them out they called their new fraternal association the 'Orden,' the Yiddish word for league. Later it became the United Jewish People's Order (UJPO).

The Workmen's Circle is non-political, but it is pro-labour. The branches are the Bund, the socialist party, the anarchist movement. There's a non-political English-speaking group; there are liberals and conservatives. It started in 1900 in New York, then here in Toronto in 1907.

The anarchist movement in Toronto was active. They were only about thirty members — men like Simkin, Joe Desser, Shef. They weren't bomb throwers, and they were active in the Jewish community. All good lecturers — Rudolf Rocker, Emma Goldman, Alexander Berkman. They were brought here by the anarchist movement."

Interview with Karl Langbord, May 24, 1984

John Garde & Co. *389-391 Spadina*

John Garde & Co. Ltd. was established in 1905 by John Garde (1861-1938), J.M. Statten and R.B. Mowry, sewing machine adjusters-mechanics on Queen Street East.

In 1921 they moved to 395 Spadina to serve the growing garment industry of the district. In the mid-30's they moved up the street, renovating the exterior of the shops. The company is presently operated by John Garde, grandson of the original owner. The company continues to sell and service industrial sewing machines.

Hoffman's Fruit and Vegetable, 339 Spadina, c. 1917
Interior of store with Rivka and Nathan Hoffman.
Toronto Jewish Congress Archives (1556)

Nusso Textiles, Wholesale Only, 425 Spadina, July, 1984
Peter MacCallum

429   425   421   419 417   415   413   411   409   407   405   403   401   399   397   3

**Machine Shop, Second
Floor, John Garde & Co.,
June, 1984**
Peter MacCallum

Lily Ilomaki

"We moved to the Spadina area when I was two or three and from then on we lived in seventeen different houses between College and Queen, on practically every street. We lived so close to Spadina because my father was an under-presser — a cloakmaker — and he used to walk to work and come home for lunch.

We started off with two or three rooms for my mother and father, my brother and myself. They were rented rooms, but we had our own furniture. We moved because we found cheaper quarters, or the place was too cold or the people needed the flat. We did live in one house on Baldwin Street for seven years, and we lived in another house twice. My mother always worked. As a matter of fact, I think I was one of the first kids to attend the daycare-nursery school at St. Christopher's houses during the First World War when they were set up.

I started working in a hosiery repair in 1929 when I was sixteen, after three years of high school. I worked there for a year and a half. We repaired silk hosiery with runs and invisible mending. We got a lot of our work from Simpson's — people would bring their hosiery to them for repair and they'd ship it off to us. About eight people worked there. We got the minimum wage or twelve dollars a week, which was considered pretty good.

I became a field organizer for the YCL (Young Communist League) in 1931. I was organizing through southwest Ontario — the automobile workers. Then I was down in the Peninsula, organizing either through the Workers Unity League or for the CIO, the industrial unions. The main object was to get the workers into industrial unions rather than the old craft unions. I was involved in picket lines and organizing the unemployed. You stayed in people's homes and got your food, but you didn't get paid. I saw my life's work then as a professional revolutionary — for three or four years I was an agitator. I spoke on street corners, at public meetings. I went on the great Ottawa Trek in 1935.

I was first arrested when I was fifteen on Bay Street at the American Consulate a few days

Delegates to the 1929 Young Communist League Convention, Mr. Mutt Billiard Parlour, 381 Spadina, 1929
Front row, second from the left: Fred Rose, Jennie Freed, Dora Leibovitch, Bertha Guberman, Emil Miller, William Kashton, Max Kelly. Second row third from the left: George Cotter, Carl Steinberg, Paul Phillips, John Williamson, Joe L. Farby, Oscar Ryan, Norman Freed, Tom Chopowick, Frank (Whitey) Breslov, Jack Eisen, Mike Golinsky. Third row middle: Martin Parker, Misha Korol, Minnie Blackburn, Charles A. Marriot.
Communist Party, Public Archives Canada (PA 124357)

376   378   380   382   384   386   388   390   392   394   396   398

before Sacco and Vanzetti were killed. I was charged with obstruction. We were told to stop picketing and then they arrested us. I must have been arrested ten times between 1928 and 1934 — for street meetings, picket lines and demonstrations in the Free Speech campaign.

I'll never forget the names of the Red Squad — Mann, Simpson, Mulholland, and Nursey the chief. I had them behind my heels many times; they knew us personally. Once we were arrested for sedition, for leafletting in front of a factory. But Judge Denton dismissed the case. When you were arrested, you were rarely charged. They just wanted to intimidate you and take you into the police station.

After 1934 I was back in Toronto, learning a trade as a machine operator on skirts. I realized I had to learn a trade to earn a living. Then when the war came I went to work on men's uniforms, about 1939-40."

Interview with Lily Ilomaki, April, 1985

May Day Parade, c. 1951
Looking southwest to Nassau Street. Joe Salsberg, the MPP for St. Andrew's, is on the far right.

Kenny Collection, Fisher Rare Book Room, University of Toronto

400   402   404   406   408   410   412   414   416   418   420   422   424   426   428   430

Grossman's Cafeteria, c. 1953
The original two houses are visible on the second and third floors.
Liquor licence application photograph, LCBO Collection, Ontario Archives

Grossman's *377-379 Spadina*

The southeast corner of Cecil and Spadina was originally developed in the late 1880's as two large houses. In the early 1950's these houses were converted into a restaurant and a new front was added. Grossman's Cafeteria was a kosher-style restaurant that seated two hundred and was run by the Grossman family with Al Grossman as manager.

Grossman's was one of the first taverns in Toronto to obtain a liquor licence — not a simple procedure in the 1950's. An application was first made in 1953 for a dining licence. This was denied because of objections by the United Church's board of evangelism and social service and the minister of the Church of All Nations (United) on Queen Street. After applying again in 1954 and 1955, Grossman's finally received a liquor licence in 1957.

> "We took the two big houses and converted them into a tavern. You couldn't build at that time — there was a restriction on buildings during the war — so all we could do was tear out the insides and leave the main structure. When we opened there was quite a large Jewish community and they started moving away. Then we had the Hungarians come through. They were the so-called Freedom Fighters. They created a whole new culture around

Spadina Avenue. Now we started off with the music. We had gypsy fiddlers and singers and our clientele, I would say, was mostly Hungarian. Then the 'hippie movement' started to come in to the area because of the large homes on Cecil Street, Beverley Street and Baldwin. And they started a complete new culture! And that's when we started going in for rock 'n roll and blues. We started off with a group called the Downchild Blues Band and he's still around, Donny Walsh. They were our house band. Then we had our so-called draft-dodgers — I used to say 'political exiles' — it was a tremendous brain-drain when they came up here from the States. You had your professors, teachers, artists and musicians. Local artists like G. Raynor, Bob Markle, John McGregor and Gershon Iskowitz started coming in also. We were one of the first to employ a black bar man. Unfortunately at the time we were chastised by the liquor board inspector. He came in and said, 'I see you have some black people working for you.' I said, 'I don't see they're black, I can't tell their colour' because as far as I was concerned there were no problems." (Al Grossman, April 30, 1984)

The Grossman family sold the bar in 1975. It continues to operate under the original name.

429   425   421   419 417   415   413   411   409   407   405   403   401   399   397

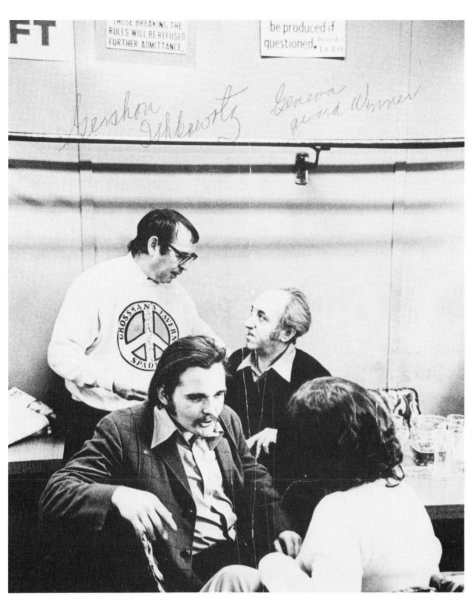

Hanging Out at Grossman's, c. 1968
Clockwise: Al Grossman, wearing the famous Grossman's peace symbol logo designed by Gary LeDrew, Gershon Iskowitz, John McGregor and unidentified woman.
Al Grossman

Draft Beer on Tap, Grossman's Tavern, 1971
From the left: Al Grossman, Sandy Mallinsky and Harold King, waiter. Grossman's was the first bar in Toronto to serve draft beer in jugs.
Al Grossman

The Only Way to Live

"European workers who settled in this country tried to earn a living and create a new homeland. The majority of the Jewish workers who came to Canada started to work in shops. They immediately recognized that to earn a real living, one had to fight for better working conditions, for conditions were very bad! But there were political differences, particularly between the left and the right.

All these activities that started for a better living, went hand-in-hand with improving the education and intellectual life of the newcomers. This helped to develop a new and active labour movement that could not have taken place without these features.

The style of life of those years was different. Many people didn't even have their own homes. Some couldn't even afford a flat; they used to live two or three in a room. ... Therefore the movement, no matter which movement you belonged to — left or right — became a *second* home.

A worker came back from work at 6 o'clock or 7 o'clock (in those days you used to work more than eight hours). After he washed and had supper and if his wife had a babysitter, then he would immediately go out. We had different kinds of places — D'Arcy Street and the Labor Lyceum, the Alhambra Hall at 450 Spadina.

You *had* to get out. Because this was the only

Industrial Union of Needle Trade Workers, Second Convention, May, 1931
Seated from the left: ?, Norman Cowan (Koza), ?, Max Schur, ?, Annie Buller, Tom McEwan, ?, Max Dolgoy, Myer Kleig, Pearl Wedro, Joshua Gershman, Jim Blugerman, Louis Goodis. Second row: Kieva Goldman (Montreal), ?, ?, Becky Luft, ?, ?, Snider, ?, ?, Switzer, ?, Oscar Ryan, Bill Sidney Levitt, Jack Berenstein (Montreal), Jenney B. (?). Third row: ?, ?, Sam Eisner, J.B. Salsberg, Dora Eckel, Sam Carr, Hannah Klinestein, Bessie Kleig, Price, Hilda Reiss (Sheiff), Louie Guberman, Izzie Minster, Sam Kagan, Mini Erlich. Fourth row: ?, Philip Halpern, Celia Gershman, Bella Issen, ?, Mina Schur, Max Kilonofsky, Rae Watson, Jimmy Meslin, Fanny Sukia.
Trade union photograph, Joshua Gershman, Multicultural History Society, Ontario Archives (218)

376   378   380   382   384   386   388   390   392   394   396   398

way to *live*. So it created a new character, a new type, a new kind of conscientious worker that combined the desire to make a nice living and get married and have children and give them an education.

Everything they were thinking led towards building a new life, bringing about a socialist system of society."

Interview with Joshua Gershman, June 30, 1984

Activists in the Fur Workers Union, Vacant Lot, Oxford and Spadina, 1926
Kneeling on the left: Max Federman. Standing third from left: Joe Dordick. The unidentified man kneeling is holding a copy of *Der Kampf*, later the *Wochenblatt*.
Multicultural History Society, Ontario Archives (MSR 9171 #15)

Activists at the Second Convention of the Industrial Needle Trade Workers, c. 1930
Left front: Bella Issen, Bella Hersac, Celia Gershman, ?. Standing centre: Sophie Mandel (nee Kates), Sarah Silver, ?. Rear: ?, ?, ?, Guberman, ?, ?.
Joshua Gershman, Multicultural History Society, Ontario Archives (239)

400   402   404   406   408   410   412   414   416   418   420   422   424   426   428   430

**J. Grossman & Co., 402
Spadina, April, 1955**
Toronto Telegram, Canada Wide

**Ontario Dry Goods &
Dresses, 374 Spadina,
c. 1920**
Morris Melamed, proprietor,
with his two daughters.
Baldwin Room, Metro Reference
Library (964-1)

420   422   424   426   428   430   436   440

Ornaments, June, 1984
East side of Spadina, north
of Cecil.
Peter MacCallum

**Victor Goodman, Victor
Goodman Furs, 458
Spadina, c. 1940**
Victor Goodman Furs has
been on Spadina since the
1920's. It is presently
located at 254 Spadina.
David Goodman

The El Mocambo *462-464 Spadina*

Built in the 1880s, the three-storey building originally opened as a dry-goods store. A barber shop, sub post office, Hunt's confectionery and Brown's Grill were located there in the early 1900s. It was renamed the El Mocambo in 1948, and re-opened with a liquor licence and the famous neon palm tree.

Mike Baird and Tom Kristenbrun bought the building in 1972, and used the upstairs bar as a venue for major national and international music and comedy acts. John Belushi, Blondie, The Cars, Elvis Costello, Fats Domino, Ritchie Havens, Murray McLauchlan, Rough Trade, Tina Turner, Buffy Saint Marie, Grover Washington and the Tom Robinson Band have all played

there. The downstairs bar usually hires local bands and is renowned for drawing capacity crowds night after night.

'The Elmo', as it is known locally, was a major news story in March 1977, when Margaret Trudeau, the wife of the prime minister, appeared as a guest of the Rolling Stones for an invitation-only taping before a live audience.

154

420   422   424   426   428   430   436   440

Paramount Hotel *337 Spadina*

The present Paramount House Tavern at Baldwin Street was built in the early 1960's. Originally it was located at D'Arcy Street, and was known as the Paramount Kosher Hotel.

Like Grossman's, one block north, the Paramount developed a local music scene and a variety of well-known regulars in the late 60's. It also became a favoured drinking spot for local and Maritime blacks.

A notorious baseball game initiated at the Paramount took place in Ramsden Park in 1967. The game involved local bikers and the regulars and black waiters from both Grossman's and the Paramount. After fifteen innings, it was not entirely clear who had won the game, but the bikers declared victory.

Paramount Hotel, June, 1984
Mural by Charles Fowler (1978).
Peter MacCallum

Outside 448 Spadina, February, 1984
David Levine

446   448   450   454   458   460   462   466½

The Alhambra *450 Spadina*

The storefront and second-floor auditorium were built in the 1880's. Walker McBean and Co., Drygoods, a "quality retail outlet," occupied the store. In the Broadway Hall upstairs, groups such as the Church of Christ, the Women's Christian Temperance Union and the International Order of Oddfellows met. There were also a few residential tenants and a music teacher.

As the area changed, the focus of activities shifted to the Jewish community. On May Day, 1918, "Men and Women Who Work in the Factory, Mill or Workshop" were invited to celebrations at the Broadway Hall, to "celebrate our Russian comrades' glorious victory in the overthrow of the barbarous despotism of Russian Nobility....With the international solidarity of labor established, then, and only then, will liberty triumph."

In the 1920's, Jewish left-wing groups were the main tenants. The Labor League, organized in June, 1926, held branch meetings, lectures and socials. The Workers Sports Association also used the auditorium as a gymnasium.

A "Free Speech Conference" was held at the hall in January, 1929. It was organized to protest the police edict that prohibited the use of any language other than English at public meetings. Representatives of fifty-five organizations attended. The protest was endorsed by Rev. Salem Bland, J.S. Woodsworth, Stanley Knowles and Jimmie Simpson, the former mayor of Toronto.

In the 1930's the name was changed to the Spadina Concert Hall; however, it was still known locally as the Alhambra. The main floor was sub-divided. Part was used as a shoe-shine shop; the second floor became a billiards parlour in the 1940's. The building is presently occupied by ABC-Cash & Carry, wholesalers.

Nodelman Sisters, Nodelman's Lunch Room, 446 Spadina, c. 1926
The Nodelman Lunch Room was a popular spot for people attending the Alhambra Hall next door.
Marion Magnusson (nee Nodelman)

420   422   424   426   428   430   436   440

The Labor League

"I was active all my life in the union, the Labor League, the left-wing movement. The city committee of the Labor League would have representatives from all the branches — some branches would be as big as 100, some 50 to 60. You would join the Labor League where you had friends, so you would be in that branch together.

It was a different relationship then. We all came from the old country, even the Ukrainians and the Poles. Each one had organizations to belong to, so when you belong to an organization you become close like a family.

Most people who worked in shops never wanted their children to work in the shops. You can't find a Jewish cloakmaker now. They always hoped that their children should have an easier life than they did. They worked hard to let their children become professionals — doctors, lawyers, teachers. Once they had an education, they could have an easier life. There are very few Jewish workers on Spadina now. They're mainly Polish, Italian, Chinese, Portuguese."

Interview with Sophie Mandel, May 27, 1984

MEN and WOMEN WHO WORK
in the Factory Nill or Workshop

YOU ARE NVITED TO ATTEND THE

:: MAY DAY ::
CELEBRATION
in
BROADWAY HALL
450 SPADINA AVE.
MAY 1st 1918

AT 2.30 P.M. and 7.30 P.M.

SEVERAL WELL KNOWN SPEAKERS WILL ADDRESS THESE CONFERENCES

May Day Leaflet, 1918
Kenny Collection, Fisher Rare Book Room, University of Toronto (Box 11, 179)

City Committee, Labor League, 1935
Representatives from eight branches. Seated from the left: Strausuner, Charles Starman, Ida Milton, Sam Lipschitz, Joe Klinestein, Harry Holtzman, Moishe Starkman. Second row: Moishe Zarin, Fishel Black, Rose Friedman, Sam Luft, Mary Harris, Charles Rosen, Sara Schwartz, Sam Rosenberg. Third row: Eva Lutsky (Zaglin), Harry Levine, Rose Boshover, Abbie Cohen Luft, Mrs. Levine, Jack Weisbord. Fourth row: Max Grafstein, Moishe Goldstein, Abbie Gross, Izzie Grubie, A. Borenstein.
Toronto Jewish Congress Archives (257)

1935

157

Roof Gardens, 1984
Second- and third-floor
apartments, east side of
Spadina south of College.
Peter MacCallum

158

Presentation of Colours, Spadina Common, July 6, 1863
Spadina Common was on the east side south of College. Presentation of the ladies of Toronto to the 10th Regiment, later the Royal Grenadiers.
Engraving from *Canadian Illustrated News*, July 25, 1863, Baldwin Room, Metro Reference Library (T 13235)

Spadina, c. 1954
Looking northeast to College.
J.V. Salmon, Baldwin Room, Metro Reference Library (S 1-374)

21   419 417   415   413   411   409   407   405   403   401   399   397   395   393   389-91

Pidyan Ha'Ben Celebration, Belvin Catering Hall, College Street, late 1930's
A banquet in honour of Joe and Millie Shanfield's son.
Toronto Jewish Congress Archives (2922)

Gay Pride Festival, 58 Cecil (now Cecil Street Community Centre), August, 1972
The festival was organized by the Community Homophile Association of Toronto (CHAT).
Al Grossman

160

 כבלות כהנו
אל תעזבנו

 אל תשליכנו
לעת זקנה

Remember
Us
and God
will
Remember
You

Remember
Us
and God
will
Remember
You

פארגעסט ניט אונז אלטיטשקע, וועט גאט אין אייך ניט פארגעסען

Toronto Jewish Old Folks Home, 23-25 Cecil
Demolished in the late 1960's, the building was

replaced by trade union offices.
Toronto Jewish Congress Archives (255)

1   419 417   415   413   411   409   407   405   403   401   399   397   395   393   389-91

College and Spadina

"How in the world I ever managed to grow up at College and Spadina, in that place in that time, I'll never know.

I was, first of all, a very impressionable kid, and since I can't honestly say that school taught me a hell of a lot, what I learned I picked up by watching the grown-ups around me. And what a collection of adults for a kid like me to take his cues from, with my parents bootleggers, my aunt and my grandmother bootleggers, one of my uncles also outside the law as a professional gambler, a cousin having done time for what the law came within a whisker of calling murder, another in-law so mixed up with the criminal element (the Purple Gang, no less) that he spent a solid year in hiding, in fear of his life, and the street itself swarming with citizens of the most dubious legitimacy, each of them polishing up his own little corner of the action.

It's funny how your memory plays tricks on you. When I sort out in my mind the denizens of The Corner from the days of my youth, all I can remember are the Rogues' Gallery types. But I know perfectly well that not everybody was a candidate for the police blotter, there had to be some solid citizens in the crowd. My uncles Yancha and Chaskel, for instance, spent their lives in solid respectability in the needle trade that was the lifeblood of lower Spadina Avenue. Lou Chesler, the multi-millionaire financier with interests all over the world, was a College and Spadina product. So was Toronto's first Jewish

Homestead Restaurant, College and Spadina, 1950's
Newspaper photograph for a crime story, Toronto Telegram, Canada Wide

420   422   424   426   428   430   436   440

mayor, Nathan Phillips, for whom our City Hall square is named. So was Spike Tenney, tough as nails then, rich as Croesus now. Our present super-mayor, Metro Toronto Chairman Paul Godfrey, grew up in my old neighbourhood, as did Mel 'Bad Boy' Lastman, Mayor of North York.

The ghetto itself was a great place for spawning nicknames, too. Max Applebaum was known as Maxie Apples, and Max Appleby as Maxie Chicago. The Brodkin brothers were always known as the Daddy Brothers, Big Daddy and Little Daddy. There was Gimpy the Athlete (who was not gimpy but a fine athlete); Pork Chops (who wasn't all there, but who was loved for what was there); Cocksy (who was all there); and Joe the Goof (who goofed about as often as a computer).

There was 'Little Itch' Leiberman, who sold papers at Queen and Yonge for a hundred years. And there was Squarehead, who ran a slophouse called the Taxi Grill, which was a favorite pre-war hangout of characters like Joe the Hobo and Danny the Indian. And what about Ya Punchick? He lived his whole life by that name without anyone ever knowing how he got it, or what it meant."

Call me Sammy, Sammy Luftspring with Brian Swarbrick, Prentice-Hall, Scarborough, 1975.

Crest Grill, 484 Spadina, July, 1984
Formerly the Crescent, the Crest is a renowned local hang-out.
Peter MacCallum

446   448   450   454   458   460   462   466½

**Stables, Baldwin and
Spadina, July, 1984**
Peter MacCallum

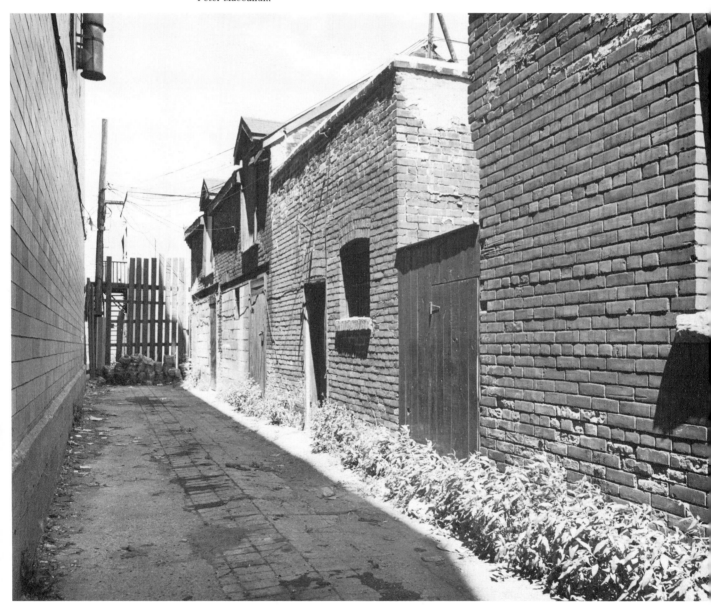

441 439 437 435 433 431 429

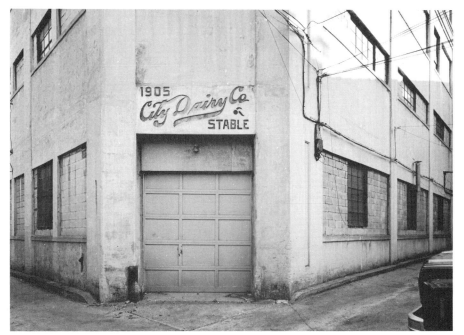

City Dairy Stables, June, 1984
The stables, built in 1905, were located in the alley southwest of College and Spadina close to the City Dairy on Spadina Crescent. They were built with a special elevator for the horses and also housed the milk delivery wagons.
Peter MacCallum

Re-laying Streetcar Tracks, May, 1927
Looking southwest from College and Spadina.
Toronto Transit Commission (4924)

1   419   417   415   413   411   409   407   405   403   401   399   397   395   393   389-91

Kensington

"Elm Place now was spelled out on a white metal plate on a post, in black letters in English and in Chinese. I reflected that my husband would be no more enamored of the resplendent Lucky Dragon on the corner than he had been of the Workmen's Labor League it replaced, the latter having been a pinochle-playing retreat for tired men whom Zbigniew accused of communist subversion, whereas I thought the only danger to society was in a slight redundancy in the name. Two blocks down, Elm Place crossed Kensington Avenue where once, when I was nine, I searched for the statue of Peter Pan. The old narrow houses still stood, separated only by painted drainpipes, but what had been parlors, inviolate, smelling of camphor and wax, never used except for weddings and funerals — these had been broken into and converted into stores. The tiny lawns were gone, their space taken up with crates of fruit and vegetables and barrels of pickles and herring. Guardians in heavy sweaters and thick boots stood out on the sidewalks. I saw their bare hands were blue with cold as they put money in the left pocket and made change out of the right pocket.

Number Forty was a bakery. Bread and rolls had been tossed onto an oilcloth-covered incline and had accumulated at the window's outer edges. As I opened the door, a bell was touched off: a superfluous summons: a woman was already waiting behind the counter. She was seated on a high stool, hunched over a newspaper spread out on the glass counter. One hand hovered over a large brass cash register; her other hand held a corner of the newspaper, ready to turn the page. She was taking her time acknowledging my presence. Finally she raised her head, gave me a quick glance and said, You're back, and continued reading. Perhaps she did know me, we were about the same age, although her face was more lined than mine and her hands work-worn. We might even have gone to Ryerson Public School at the same time.

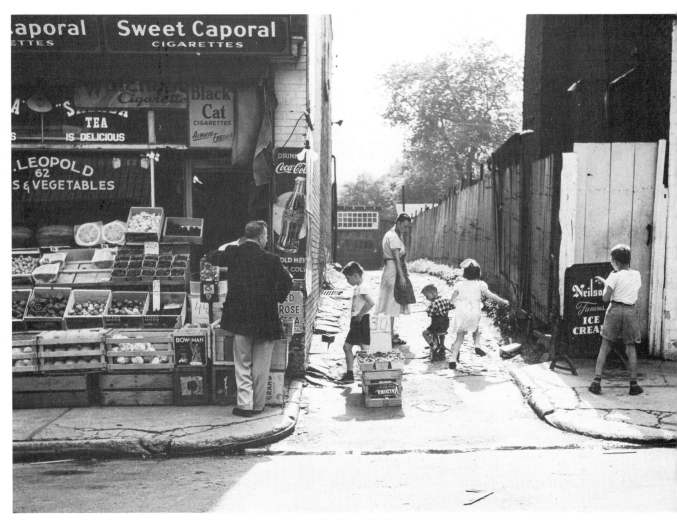

A. Leopold Fruits &
Vegetables, Kensington
Market, 1955
Michel Lambeth, Public
Archives Canada

Watermelons, Smelts and
Milk Herring, Kensington
Market, 1955
Michel Lambeth, Public
Archives Canada

I circled the small store, pretending to be making up my mind. ...Even though her eyes never left the newspaper, I sensed the woman was taking my measure. I wished I had on a printed rayon dress with a clean printed cotton apron over it, as she was wearing. I regretted being dressed in my black dress, the tailored tweed coat, the pearls. If you have grown up in these streets it is the act of a traitor to return smelling of expensive perfume and sporting the costume of another class. It isn't going away that causes resentment: after all, out of sight, out of mind. But once out of sight, I should stay out of sight. It is an unwritten law. Not only can you not *go* home again, you must not *come* home again. I took my time, going from kaiser rolls to onion buns, picking them out of wire baskets, pinching them as is the custom, keeping some and discarding others. One by one she brushed aside my selection with her forearm. Without looking up she knew when I had fin-ished. She stopped reading, took a paper bag from under the counter, threw in the rolls, all the while shaking her head in what seemed to be disapproval. At what I had chosen? Still not looking at me she asked,

– What else?

Behind her was a wall of shelves laden with breads.

– What kind of bread have you got?

– White, black, *chalah*, Russian black, rye, double rye, with seeds, without seeds, water bread. What do you want?

– Give me a quarter of Russian black.

Just as she turned to the shelf behind her, I detected a hint of triumph on her face. She had seen through me: I had tipped my hand: only those familiar with the enormous proportions of a Russian black bread know to ask for a segment. She cut through the thick crust, leaning heavily on the long knife. ..."

Basic Black with Pearls, Helen Weinzweig, Anansi, Toronto, 1980.

Augusta Avenue,
Kensington Market area,
1955
Michel Lambeth, Public
Archives Canada

The Communist Party

"At that time the Communist Party was alive
and well, and they would try and give out leaflets and speak in the park and try to explain the
issues. What it meant to people — solidarity and
sticking together and things like that.

There were blacks in the Communist Party.
They were recruiting a lot among young people.
We would go to dances and things like that.
They had a place. Where you come down Belle-
vue, there's a park on the left hand side. Well,
that big house, before you make the turn. We
came from a dance at the Hall (United Negros
Improvement Association on College), to where
there were the Communist Party dances. Just a
dance, and that was where they'd try to get you
involved, indoctrinate you, or try to sign you up
for a card.

I don't know why people make such a big
deal of it. Now it's a big scare tactic. They're
people. Big deal, so they're Communist! Listen,
as a young person there's no jobs for you, you'll
listen to anyone, you got the time, this is basic.
When you got a job you're rushing here, rushing

Kensington Market, 1955
Michel Lambeth, Public
Archives Canada

168

**Rudolph Family Seder,
77 Oxford, early 1940's**
Seated from the left: Mac,
Estelle, Picus and Tovi
Rudolph, Sam, Mary and
Harry.
Toronto Jewish Congress
Archives (526)

**Old Clothes Mart,
Kensington Market area,
December, 1922**
John Boyd, Public Archives
Canada (84968)

there. There were no jobs. So you have time!
You listen. You want to talk? Talk! Basically
they tried to give working people direction.
They tried to get unions into non-union places.
People got beaten. The cops came in. Trying to
get a standard wage. Now it's common, people
think nothing of it."

Interview with Ernie Richardson, May 27, 1984

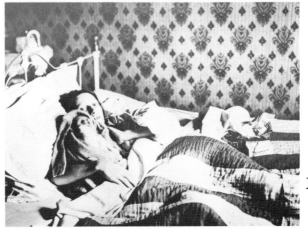

Kensington Avenue, 1910
Mother and child after
home birth.
Health department record, City
of Toronto Archives (Series 32,
#312)

Broadway Methodist Tabernacle *445 Spadina*

The Spadina Avenue Methodist Church congregation purchased this site for $4,000 in 1876. The congregation's original frame church, at the corner of St. Patrick (Dundas) and Spadina, was moved up the Avenue on rollers. In 1879 the cornerstone was laid for a new brick church which cost $16,000 and seated 900 people — "a handsome edifice in 'first-pointed' or Early English Gothic — most comfortably provided with elegantly covered pews, a choir for the singers, and a beautifully formed pulpit." (*Toronto: Past and Present until 1882*, P. Mulvany, 1884.)

The structure was partially demolished in 1887. A new church was designed by E.J. Lennox, the architect who was simultaneously working on the design for the new City Hall on Terauley (Bay) Street. It was modelled after the Bond Street Congregational Church; a section of the original frame structure was added into the new building as the "Tabernacle." The church opened in May, 1889. It later changed its name to Broadway Methodist Tabernacle, after the area from College to Bloor known locally as "Broadway."

The Broadway Methodist Tabernacle was one of the most active and important churches in the city. Dr. Salem Bland, who lived at 554 Spadina Crescent and was known for his attacks on fundamentalism and his support of labour, preached there from 1919-23.

As the Anglo-Saxon community moved north in the early 1900's, the church declined in importance. After the unification of the Methodist, Presbyterian and Congregational churches in 1925, the Broadway Methodist Tabernacle was demolished.

In 1934 a new four-storey Medico-Dental Building, designed by architect Benjamin Brown, opened. For many years the roof had a huge Neilsen's Jersey Milk Chocolate sign, which was a local landmark. Tip Top Tailors continues to occupy the corner store, along with a German bookstore and Benny's Barbershop.

Broadway Methodist Tabernacle, c. 1891
M. Micklethwaite, Public Archives Canada (RD 550)

Spadina, c. 1870
Looking northeast to Spadina Crescent. The house on the northeast corner of Russell and Spadina Crescent was owned by Sir Adam Wilson.
Baldwin Room, Metro Reference Library (T 12794)

College and Spadina, c. 1900
Looking northwest to the Crescent. The streetcar is changing horses (a fresh horse is feeding around the corner). The sandwich board is advertising a Salvation Army "Moonlight Excursion."
City engineer photograph, City of Toronto Archives (Vol. 5, 63)

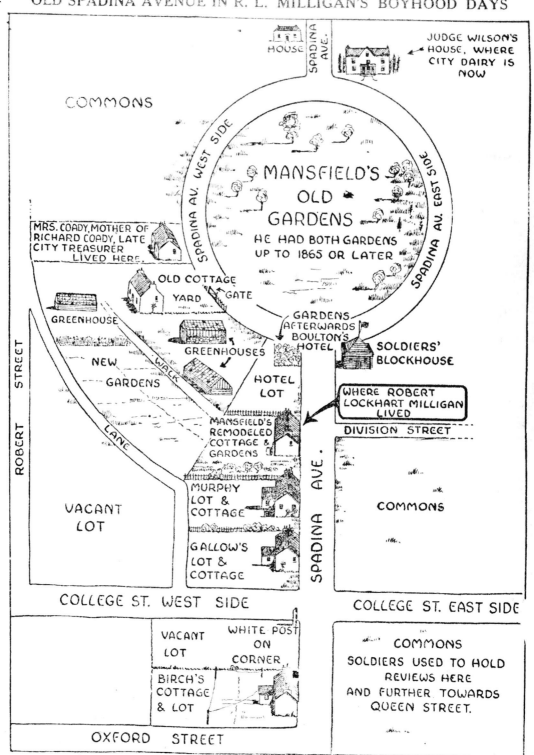

HOUSE

JUDGE WILSON'S HOUSE, WHERE CITY DAIRY IS NOW

COMMONS

SPADINA AV. WEST SIDE

SPADINA AV. EAST SIDE

MANSFIELD'S OLD GARDENS
HE HAD BOTH GARDENS UP TO 1865 OR LATER

MRS. COADY, MOTHER OF RICHARD COADY, LATE CITY TREASURER LIVED HERE.

OLD COTTAGE YARD GATE

GREENHOUSE

WALK

GREENHOUSES

GARDENS AFTERWARDS BOULTON'S HOTEL

SOLDIERS' BLOCKHOUSE

NEW GARDENS

LANE

ROBERT STREET

HOTEL LOT

MANSFIELD'S REMODELED COTTAGE & GARDENS

WHERE ROBERT LOCKHART MILLIGAN LIVED

DIVISION STREET

VACANT LOT

MURPHY LOT & COTTAGE

COMMONS

SPADINA AVE.

GALLOW'S LOT & COTTAGE

COLLEGE ST. WEST SIDE

COLLEGE ST. EAST SIDE

VACANT LOT

WHITE POST ON CORNER

COMMONS SOLDIERS USED TO HOLD REVIEWS HERE AND FURTHER TOWARDS QUEEN STREET.

BIRCH'S COTTAGE & LOT

OXFORD STREET

This sketch map by the veteran actor recalls the time when market gardens flourished at what is now the geographical heart of Toronto.

Mansfield's Old Gardens, c. 1860
Illustration drawn from memory by R.L. Milligan, for the future site of Knox College. Toronto *Telegram*, December 23, 1927. Baldwin Room, Metro Reference Library

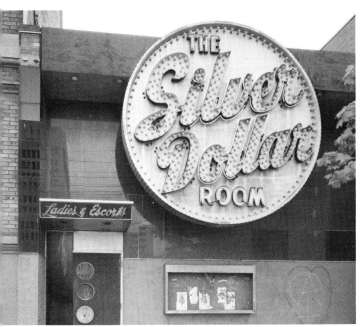

Silver Dollar, July, 1984
The cocktail lounge of the
Waverley Hotel, often
called "The Buck."
Peter MacCallum

**Spadina from the
Crescent, May, 1927**
Looking south, before the
street was widened.
Public works photograph,
J.V. Salmon, City of Toronto
Archives (2010)

Waverley Hotel *484 Spadina*

This location was originally Robert Milligan's market garden. By 1870 it was the site of "four small rough-cast cottages." In 1882 they were demolished and a branch of the local YMCA was built.

In 1900 J.J. Powell built the Waverley House. It was enlarged in 1925. The Toronto Tourist and Convention Association located there in the late 1920's. A lounge licence was awarded in 1955, and the Silver Dollar bar was added in 1958.

The clientele of the Waverley has shifted with the local community; predominantly Jewish, Hungarian and black in the 1950's, it is now favoured by urban native people and street people. Murray McLauchlan's song, "Queen of the Silver Dollar," described the local scene:

> I walked down to Kensington Market
> Bought me a fish to fry
> I went to the Silver Dollar
> Looked a stranger in the eye
> A friend of mine says
> That he don't think this town's so out of sight
> But he's got shades all around his soul
> And he thinks he's seen the light.

502

508

Scott Mission *502-504 Spadina*

The Scott Mission began in 1912 at Elm and Elizabeth streets as a "Presbyterian Mission to the Hebrew People of Toronto." It was known as the Christian Synagogue and tried to convert local Jews to Christianity (with no apparent success). It was renamed the Scott Institute in 1921. The mission was directed by Morris Zeidman, a Jewish convert to Christianity and a graduate of Knox College.

During the Depression the Mission started a soup kitchen and did relief work for the city's destitute. In 1941 Zeidman came under attack from the Presbyterian Church for his concentration on relief, rather than the evangelical work among the Jewish community which was supposed to be the Mission's primary activity.

Zeidman resigned his position as director and in November, 1941, opened the Scott Mission at 724-726 Bay Street, under the banner "non-denominational/strongly evangelical."

The Mission moved to 502 Spadina in 1948. The old premises were torn down in 1960 and a new building was erected.

The Zeidman family is still involved, and the Mission continues to assist needy men and women.

In 1983 it provided 220,161 hot meals to men and women, 24,545 people with groceries, 7,224 families with free clothing, 55,135 Meals on Wheels, 4,300 Christmas hampers, 896 Christmas toys for children, and sent 631 children to Caledon Camp.

Morning Line-up, Scott Mission, November, 1953
Canadian Tribune, Public Archives Canada (PA 93921)

Outside the Scott Mission, November, 1953
The reporter on the right is interviewing several men.
Canadian Tribune, Public Archives Canada (PA 93923)

Becky Buhay Funeral Procession, 1953
Looking south to the Medico-Dental Building. Becky Buhay was an activist and leader in the Communist Party in the 1930's and 40's. The buildings on the left were demolished in the early 1960's, to be replaced by an underground garage ramp for the Clarke Institute of Psychiatry.
Communist Party, Public Archives Canada (PA 127685)

502

508

City Dairy *563 Spadina Crescent*
The City Dairy, built on the northeast quadrant
of Spadina Crescent in 1900, advertised itself as
the newest and cleanest "pasteurized" dairy in
the city. It was designed by G.M. Miller, who
also designed the City Dairy stables in the southwest alley at College and Spadina. In full operation the dairy employed 257 people, primarily
Italians who lived in the vicinity. In 1929 the
dairy was acquired by the U.S.-based Borden's
Dairy, which had recently established itself in
Canada. Borden's also operated a retail ice
cream outlet from the building, which was
marked by a huge milk bottle on the roof. The
dairy ceased operations in the 1950's, and the
building was bought by the University of Toronto. A number of university departments, including the sculpture studios, the sociology
department and the forestry laboratories, have
occupied the building since then.

City Dairy, c. 1906
From *Toronto the Prosperous,
1872-1906*, Baldwin Room,
Metro Reference Library

**Lobby and Stairway,
Borden Building, 1984**
Peter MacCallum

**Forestry Department
Laboratory, Borden Build-
ing, Spadina Crescent,
1984**
Peter MacCallum

Lansdowne School *Spadina Crescent*

Lansdowne School opened in March, 1888. It was intensely crowded, with 945 students in twelve rooms. Additions were built in 1889 and 1909.

In 1913 the school was damaged by fire and partially rebuilt. With the purchase of more property on Robert Street, a new school was opened in 1961, and the old building was demolished. The name was changed to Lord Lansdowne School, to avoid confusion with another school on Lansdowne Avenue.

The present school was designed by the Board of Education architectural and engineering staff. The Board of Education minutes pointed out that the round building design was "not the result of a desire to be different, but rather to produce a most economical and functional building both from the standpoint of the building itself as well as consideration of land usage. Because of the shape of the building, a saving of approximately 7,000 sq. ft. of actual floor area was realized." (March 16, 1967)

Lansdowne Public School, c. 1900
M. Micklethwaite, Public Archives Canada (RD 632)

178

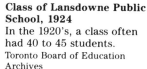

Class of Lansdowne Public School, 1924
In the 1920's, a class often had 40 to 45 students.
Toronto Board of Education Archives

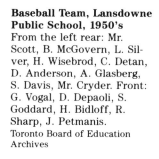

Baseball Team, Lansdowne Public School, 1950's
From the left rear: Mr. Scott, B. McGovern, L. Silver, H. Wisebrod, C. Detan, D. Anderson, A. Glasberg, S. Davis, Mr. Cryder. Front: G. Vogal, D. Depaoli, S. Goddard, H. Bidloff, R. Sharp, J. Petmanis.
Toronto Board of Education Archives

The Children of Our New Immigrants

"It is apparent that the government on account of the large immigration we are to receive, must give very close attention to the education of the masses, not only with the view of developing a Canadian spirit, a love for our country and an appreciation of our system of government, but also so far as possible to inoculate our new citizens with the spirit of the empire. The children of our new immigrants, in the natural course of events, may be expected to become good Canadians, but it will require education if they are to appreciate the advantages of imperial unity so patent to most of us who come from British stock."

A.D. McRae, "Canadian Citizenship of the Future," *Proceedings of the Canadian Club of Toronto, 1919-20*, Toronto, 1921. Quoted in *The Immigrants*, R. Harney & H. Troper, Van Nostrand Reinhold, Toronto, 1975.

Salem Bland *554 Spadina Crescent*
The house at 554 Spadina Crescent was owned for over thirty years by Salem Bland, a well-known Methodist, social gospel minister and writer. Bland moved to Toronto in 1919, when he was engaged by the Broadway Methodist Tabernacle congregation at College and Spadina. In 1926 he accepted a position with the Western Congregational congregation. They had formerly been located at 327 Spadina, but had sold the church to the Hebrew Men of England Synagogue.

Bland was a columnist for the Toronto *Daily Star* in the 1930's and 40's, writing under the title "The Observer." He died at his home in 1950.

Salem Bland
Painting by Lawren S.
Harris, 1925.
Toronto Daily Star donation, Art
Gallery of Ontario

**Northwest Quadrant,
Spadina Crescent, 1984**
Peter MacCallum

Dr. Emily Howard Stowe and Dr. Augusta Stowe-Gullen

The original house at 461 Spadina Crescent was the home of Dr. Emily Howard Stowe, the first woman to practise medicine in Canada. Her daughter, Dr. Augusta Stowe-Gullen, and her husband, Dr. John Gullen, also physicians, lived at 463 Spadina Crescent.

In 1876 Emily Stowe helped form the Toronto Women's Literary Club (later the Toronto Women's Suffrage Association), one of the earliest suffrage organizations in Canada. They campaigned for the right of women to vote in municipal elections, admittance for women to the University of Toronto, and separate washrooms for women in factories. Dr. Stowe was a founder of the Ontario Medical College for Women, the clinics of which evolved into the present Women's College Hospital.

Augusta Stowe-Gullen followed in her mother's footsteps as the first woman to graduate from a Canadian medical school. She practised from her home on Spadina Crescent and worked at the newly opened Western Hospital on Bathurst Street. She was president of the Dominion Women's Enfranchisement Association and its successor, the Canadian Suffrage Association.

In April, 1917, the suffrage campaign was victorious. A bill granted full suffrage to the women of Ontario.

The houses at 461 and 463 Spadina Crescent were demolished in 1962 to make way for the Clarke Institute of Psychiatry.

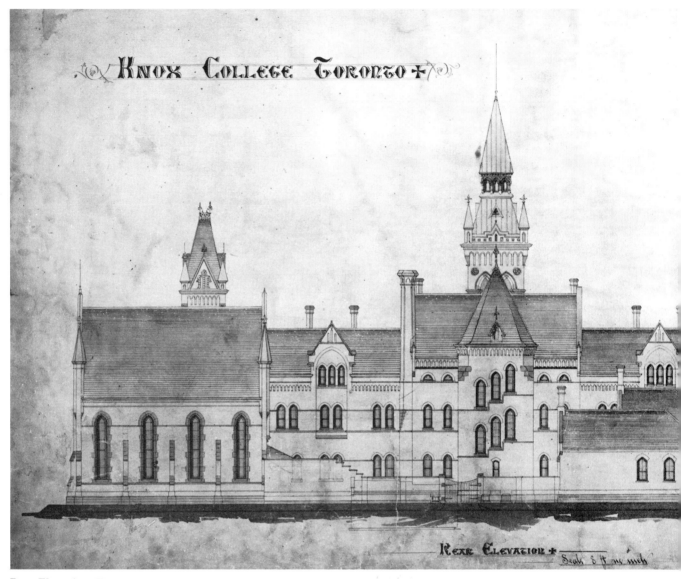

KNOX COLLEGE TORONTO

REAR ELEVATION

Rear Elevation, Knox College, 1873
Baldwin Room, Metro Reference Library (T 13001)

Knox College, September, 1926
The building was occupied by various government departments in the 1920's.
John Boyd, Public Archi Canada (PA 87502)

Spadina Crescent

Spadina Crescent first appeared on city maps in 1838. Known then as Crescent Gardens, Dr. Baldwin deeded it to the city for a park. However, his granddaughter sold it to Knox College in 1873 for $10,000. Knox College, the Presbyterian College of the University of Toronto, was built on the property at a cost of $120,000. It was designed by Smith and Gemmel and opened in 1875. It consisted of five professors' rooms, two reading rooms, a library, board room, museum, bedrooms to accommodate 100 and a dining room for 100. The first autumn, a strong wind removed an entire corner of the third storey.

In 1906 the board of management of Knox College decided to move closer to the University of Toronto campus. The 31-year-old building was

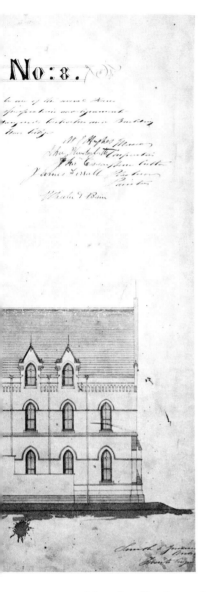

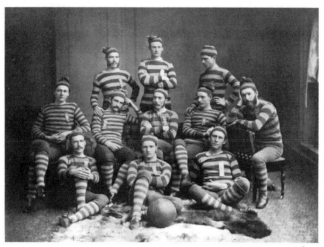

**The Metaphysical &
Literary Society and
the Soccer Team, Knox
College, 1879-80**
Knox College Archives

considered a fire hazard and inadequate for residential purposes. From 1908 to 1910 there were rumours of a major department store opening on the site. Others felt differently: "No more perfect park site can be found in the city. It is in close proximity to a large and important residential district now unprovided with a single breathing spot. Every cent spent on its beautification would 'show' and would aid in advertising Toronto, for Spadina Avenue is destined to become one of the most important thoroughfares of the city." (*News*, Oct. 9, 1906)

In 1916 the College became a military hospital and was renovated to accommodate 250 invalid soldiers. During this period Amelia Earhart, later a famed pilot, worked as a nurse's aid at the Spadina Military Hospital.

Plans were announced in 1931 to build a new arena for hockey, boxing and wrestling. The Canadian Wrecking and Construction Company was awarded a contract by the city to demolish the college in the 1930's; this was later rescinded. In 1943 the University of Toronto acquired the buildings which were eventually used by Connaught Laboratories for the production of penicillin. It was here that the first gamma globulin was produced by separating human blood into strategic components. This led to the discovery of the polio virus.

The building is presently under renovation and is used by various university departments.

671 Spadina, c. 1968
Known locally as the "bird
cage," Anansi Press was
located in the basement of
this unusual house in
1967-68.
Anansi Press

Late Victorian Sitting Room, 697 Spadina, 1893
The house was built in 1892, and the first occupant was Mr. Stracey Lake, a cashier at Gutta-Percha Rubber Manufacuring Co.
Strathy Smith, City of Toronto Archives (177)

Digger House, 115 Spadina Road, January, 1969
A "hippie haven."
Toronto Telegram, Canada Wide

Bloor and Spadina, April, 1929
Looking west on Bloor, the original Varsity Tea Room is on the right.
Transit record photograph, Public Archives Canada (PA 54863)

Organizing Committee, Jewish Art Institute, Jewish Centre, 651 Spadina, 1950
From the left rear: Dora Wechsler, Dr. Elie Borowski, Dr. Anna Gelber, Bailey Leslie. Front: Tutzi Sequin,

Mrs. Bert Cooper, Beatrice Fischer.
Toronto Telegram, York University Archives

Bloor and Spadina, August 1944
Looking south on Spadina, with a news kiosk on the southeast corner.
Transit record photograph, Public Archives Canada (PA 54026)

Demonstration Against German Re-armament, Bloor and Spadina, c. 1960
Demonstration against the revival of Nazi activity in Canada and German re-armament. Joshua

Gershman, editor of the *Wochenblatt*, in the centre.
Ontario Archives, Multicultural History Society Collection

The Spadina Ramp
Poster by Dennis Burton, 1971, from a series of posters designed for the Spadina Review Corporation.
Cameron House

Victory Party Celebrating Cancellations of the Spadina Expressway, Brunswick House, June, 1971
From the left, seated: ?, Ned Jacobs, Paul Rhinehart, Rose Smith (standing), Allan Powell (arm raised), David Steiger, Fiona Nelson, Colin Vaughan, David Nowlan (hidden), Nadina Nowlan, Jim Lemon, Ying Hope. Standing centre: Jeff Sack (striped tie). Major figures missing: Ellen Adams, Jane Jacobs.
Tibor Kolley, Globe and Mail

The Spadina Expressway

On June 4, 1971, the *Globe & Mail* published a capsule history of the Spadina Expressway project:

December, 1953: Metro Council calls for route plans of extension of Spadina Road from Dupont Street to Wilson Avenue, at estimated cost of $11.5-million.

March, 1954: Metro and North York agree to build section within North York. The Ontario Municipal Board approves $1.8-million costs in June, 1955. Road is to have no bridges.

October, 1957: Metro Council passes revised Spadina plans for within North York, calling for bridges and median subway tracks and new cost estimate of $7.2 million. The OMB approves in January, 1958, with no public opposition.

July, 1959: Metro Council agrees to build, with province, elaborate intersection of Highway 401 and unbuilt Spadina route, to serve Yorkdale shopping centre. Later, Ontario Department of Highways insists the expressway be built to Bloor Street, over objections of York and Forest Hill Councils.

December, 1959: Metro Council decides to extend Spadina route from Dupont south to Bloor Street.

Planning Board adopts first detailed plans for $67.6-million Spadina Expressway, on understanding that Crosstown and Highway 400 expressways follow it. Metro Roads Committee asks that Spadina subway line operate before the expressway.

December, 1961: City Council agrees on Spadina subway, but asks Metro to defer expressway to study if Metro can afford it and if it is a good project. Design changes, near Casa Loma, increase Spadina cost estimates another $6-million.

Dec. 12: Metro Council approves expressway and median subway space to be built from Highway 401 to Lawrence Avenue, and to refer all other aspects back to Roads Committee.

March, 1962: Metro Council adopts Roads Committee recommendation that expressway be built to Bloor, that there be no Crosstown, and that studies continue on proposed extension of expressway south to connect with Gardiner Expressway.

August, 1963: Municipal Board approves full $73.6-million expressway, Chairman J.A. Kennedy ruling that sectional interests (of York and Forest Hill Councils) must "give way to the public need of the larger area." The OMB hearings took only two days, and were considered so routine that no transcript was taken. Metro asked OMB approval for only $1-million of the estimated $79-million subway line down the expressway.

December, 1966: first section of Spadina Expressway opened, from Wilson Heights Boulevard above Highway 401 south to Lawrence, including Yorkdale-401 interchange with 23 bridges. Metro Council adopts "proposed expressway system" including Crosstown and Highway 400 expressways.

In 1967, Municipal Board authorization for Spadina costs is increased to $75.6-million. By 1968, a storm sewer built along the route and once planned to cost $1.5-million is expected to cost $13.5-million.

Early 1969: City Council and the province approve city's first Official Plan, showing the Spadina but not the Crosstown Expressway. Metro Council agrees to speed completion of the Spadina to Bloor by 1975, by delaying allotments for construction of the Scarborough Expressway. Metro Council learns cost estimates for the Spadina highway, not counting the median subway line, have risen to $136.2-million — $62-million more than submitted to the Municipal Board in 1963.

September, 1969: Because of citizen concern and roads officials' need for time to revise plans for the expressway, Metro agrees to call no more tenders for work on the expressway, pending a transportation review.

October, 1969: Formation and expansion of the Stop Spadina Save Our City Co-ordinating Committee.

January, 1970: Highways Minister George Gomme says Metro Council does not have to build Spadina to Bloor, but can stop route where it wants.

March, 1970: Metro publishes review of Spadina and transportation, saying Spadina is essential and cannot be stopped anywhere short of the College Street area. Elaborate ramps at Davenport Road are to cut need for Crosstown Expressway. Revised costs: expressway, $143-million, subway $95-million.

April, 1970: Metro Transportation Committee hears 222 briefs from citizens and groups, almost all opposed to completion of expressway and most dubious that the subway should be built along that alignment. City Council does not oppose the project, but asks that Metro, before approving project, establish an independent inquiry to determine whether the expressway and subway should be built.

June, 1970: Metro Council approves completion of expressway and subway.

September, 1970: Spadina Review Corp. is formed by citizens, who retain lawyer John Robinette to oppose Spadina before the Municipal Board. Metro then agrees to do no work on Spadina in the interim.

January, 1971: Municipal Board holds three weeks of hearings on Metro's application for more money to complete the expressway, and on Review Corporation's request that previous OMB orders of Spadina approval be rescinded.

February 17: The three-member OMB panel who heard the case deliver an unprecedented 2-1 split decision, the majority favoring completion of the project and Chairman Kennedy requesting continued halt until more studies and an "agonizing reappraisal" are completed.

Within 30 days, the citizens' Review Corporation appeals the OMB decision to the provincial Cabinet, which has power to uphold or reverse the OMB decision or order a new OMB hearing.

June 3: Cabinet rejects continuation of expressway, favours aiding rapid-transit routes.

Stop Spadina Demonstration, March, 1970
A rally and demonstration leaving Convocation Hall, University of Toronto. On the left is Art Mackelwain, President of the Engineering Society. On the right is Allan Powell.
Barrie Davis, Globe and Mail

A Note on the Exhibition

SPADINA AVE: A Photohistory
A SPACE, 204 Spadina Avenue, Toronto
August 15-September 16, 1984
Curator: Rosemary Donegan
Architectural documentation photography: Peter
  MacCallum

The exhibition was assisted by the following
agencies and foundations: Canada Council,
MacLean Foundation, Ontario Heritage Foundation, Secretary of State: Multiculturalism Canada
and Ontario Bicentennial Celebrations, Toronto
Arts Council, Toronto Sesquicentennial Ward 6
Committee, Wintario.

*Spadina Avenue Documentary Exhibition
Committee:*
Rosemary Donegan, Craig Heron, Peter
MacCallum, Doug Sigurdson **Editorial assistant:**
Renee Baert **Furniture and installation
design:** Barry Sampson **Graphic production:**
Checkmate Photographic Centre **Mounting:**
Isaac Applebaum, Pamela Gawn **Photographic
installation design:** Stan Denniston **Photo-
graphic production assistant:** Pamela Gawn
Poster Design: R.A. Gledhill **Publicity:** Louise
Garfield **A SPACE Staff:** Michael Banger,
Edward Lam, Doug Sigurdson **Text production:**
Dinah Forbes, Ross Irwin, Ormond McKague
Typesetting: Lynn Fernie **Wall construction:**
Peter Blendell

Acknowledgements

I would like to thank all those individuals and
institutions that assisted in the research and
development of the exhibition and the book.

Irving Abella
Al Abromovitch
Ken Adachi
Patricia Aldana
Bob Alexander
Moira Armour
Renee Baert
George Baird
John Joseph Benjamin
Ted Bieler
Matt Blajer
Michael Blazer
Pearl Blazer
Sarah Binks
Tom Burrows
Buzz Burza
Jick Chan
Olivia Chow
Judith Coburn
Matt Cohen
Philip Corrigan
Graham Coughtry
Development Educa-
  tion Centre
Diane Cristall
Marcia Cuthbert
Eileen Donegan
Peter Dorfman
Sylvia Draper
John Dunn
Andrew Durocevz
Ray Edwards
Shirley Faessler
Max Federman

John Foster
Ruth Frager
Douglas Franklin
Richard Fung
Brian Gee
Joshua Gershman
Victor Glickman
David Goodman
Ken Greenberg
Bill Greer
Al Grossman
Robert Harney
Alice Heap
Dan Heap
Al Hercovitch
Craig Heron
Dan Hill, Sr.
Robert Hill
Chrystyna Hnatiw
Richard Holden
Jeff House
Gurion Hyman
Lily Ilomaki
Max Ilomaki
Winnie Ing
Franc Iocovetti
Ross Irwin
Av Isaacs
Gershon Iskowitz
Jane Jacobs
Scott James
Nancy Johnson
Basil Johnston
Jude Johnston

Lennie Johnston
George Kapelos
Robert Kellerman
Bruce Kidd
David Kidd
Marty Kohn
Les Kovachi
Chris Kuziak
Herman Ladovsky
Karl Langbord
Jack Layton
Dan Leckie
Gary LeDrew
Don Lee
Josephine Lee
Karen Levine
Meryl Levine
Mike Lyons
Ormond MacKague
Catherine MacLeod
Marion Magnusson
Fatch Makos
Sophie Mandel
D'Arcy Martin
Kelly Mitchell
Roger Obonsawan
Keibo Oiwa
Andrew Patterson
Suellen Pigott
Dave Pinkus
Dan Poulos
Elizabeth Price
Gordon Raynor
John Reeves
Ernie Richardson
Bob Rodgers
Norman Rogul
Lori Rotenberg

Stella Rudolph
George Rust D'Eye
Oscar Ryan
Toby Ordon Ryan
Joe Salsberg
Rick Salutin
Paul Sannella
Lee Schecter
Mark Schekter
Annabell Schien
Allan Schwann
Dan Schwartz
John Sewell
Ben Shek
Irving Shopsowitz
Michael Solomon
Steven Speisman
Lynn Spink
Greg Spurgeon
Howard Starr
Mercedes Steedman
Lisa Steele
Allan Suddon
Tess Taconis
Sammy Taft
Julia Tao
Eleanor Thall
Michael Torosien
Tony Unitas
Jeanette Urbas
Willie Villano
Tom Wakayama
Ted Wickson
Alex Wilson
Cheryl Zimmerman

The Photography

The photographs in this book tell a story about a street and a neighbourhood. They also raise questions about historical and contemporary photographs. What does an actual photograph represent in two dimensions? What do we "read" into a photograph based on our experience of photography, Spadina Avenue, local politics, etc.? Why was a specific photograph taken? What was the intention of the photographer? What was the intention of the client/patron? Why was one specific historical photograph preserved and archived, rather than another?

The historical photographs in the book have been drawn from a variety of sources — both institutions and private collections. The images from institutions, organizations and the media tend by their nature to be formal. Their style reflects their use. For example, newspapers shoot and select photographs to illustrate an event/story. Public institutions collect images as a record of public works, immigration, police investigation and surveillance, public health,

transit and real estate development, and as advertising. Ethnic associations collect materials as a record of survival, as emblems of solidarity and as images of progress. Trade unions, churches and educational institutions collect photographs to record their own development and activities. Political parties use photographs to elucidate certain issues and philosophies, and as propaganda.

Individuals, on the other hand, take photographs and collect them for more informal purposes, as personal mementoes of family and community events and as records of ownership and achievement. They are seldom intended for use within a public context. The professional photographer selects and preserves images within particular conventions of commercial photography or "art" photography.

The photographs in this book are captioned in detail to establish the context of the photograph. They allow us to see Spadina Avenue, but, even more they help us "imagine" Spadina Avenue.

Index

191